PRAISE FOR

Life Lived in Small Moments

"Dr. Elkun is a careful observer of the turns of life: from early experiences to issues of success and failure, from midlife crises to old age and impending death, and even blissful nirvana. His accounts adeptly reach to the psychological center of these experiences and throw some wise advice and counsel over them. The book is written in a hopeful mood with most of the issues he addresses having either reasonable solutions or at least explanations. I am sure that Dr. Elkun's practice for many years as a psychotherapist and psychoanalyst has informed his writing, and for readers searching for some ways to think through the many changes to their lives, I would recommend this book."

—David Klass, MD

"Dr. Len Elkun writes about living life in all its various components and complexities. He takes us on a journey through a series of erudite yet folksy essays to explore what really matters and what we can let go of. His keen observations and insights are a rich compendium of wisdom gained from professional and personal perspectives. Clearly, he writes from a position of aging without being maudlin and without regret, but instead with wisdom and affirmation of life in all its vicissitudes. Thank you, Dr. Len!"

—Robert Rosenfeld, MD

"You may not find this an easy or fast read, but you will find a worthwhile and stimulating examination of a diverse variety of topics. You will discover at least a few themes that you not only can relate to, but also learn from. The essays are presented in a straightforward manner, but at the same time Dr. Elkun introduces us to perspectives on the topic that we may not have considered. He is very adept at expressing how human behavior is influenced and modified by the multifactorial issues imbedded in the topics he discusses.

A psychiatrist's view, understanding, and assessment—well-founded in knowledge and experience—is readily perceptible throughout. Interestingly, it is also presented in a manner that allows those of us without his experience to understand his view. Dr. Elkun gives us plenty to ponder.

Personally, I found many chapters to be inspirational, and believe they will prove to be an aspirational narrative for readers."

—Paul Teplitsky, DDS

"Dr. Elkun has provided us with a well written, thoughtful book centered around the importance of taking joy from the small daily occurrences in our lives. He writes from the perspective of someone who reflects global exposure in what he perceives to be a disturbing deterioration of our environment, and yet he provides us with optimism for the future. Dr. Elkun is clear that not everyone may agree with his assessments but there is no doubt that his assertions provide food for thought and we are stimulated to make our own assessments.

This is excellent and timely reading, particularly during our current political and public health crisis. It leaves us better equipped to make sense of our world."

—William Goodall, M.D., FACEP

LIFE LIVED
in Small Moments

LEONARD D. ELKUN, MD

Editorial and project management:
Second City Publishing Services LLC
www.secondcitypublishing.com

Book Cover Design & Layout: Summer R. Morris
www.sumodesignstudio.com

Cover Illustration: Timothy Foss

Printed in the United States of America
ISBN: 978-0-578-85413-7

To Ziki and Adella,
who brought light and lightness into our lives.

CONTENTS

PART 3: *RANDOM PERSPECTIVES*

LIFE LIVED
in Small Moments

INTRODUCTION

IN TRYING TO PIECE TOGETHER some themes for this collection of essays, in order to present a somewhat organized and logical progression for readers, the process behind the creation of these essays became front and center. I have never seen myself as a "writer" or even a high-level thinker, no doubt a function of a less than perfect childhood and a sense that carries through until this date. The process of creating these essays is best described as helter-skelter.

All of these pieces were written between mid-March and the end of August during the COVID-19 pandemic of 2020, a period in which we were all seriously shut in. During that time, each day began as did the day before and would duplicate itself the following day as well, reminiscent of the film *Groundhog Day*. But those days also gave my wife and I the gift of being able to have long and conversational breakfasts each morning. During those long and lingering breakfasts, any number of topics would come up. My wife and I have a habit of never finishing any conversation completely, instead always leaving a door open for more discussion and interpretation. Inevitably, our discussions would generate a set of ideas in my mind, and when I had time during that day

I would write down some random thoughts. Before long I had written yet another essay.

The first thing I did every time I finished an essay was to read what I had written to my wife, eager to get her feedback on the content—and probably to also gain her admiration. She provided her commentary easily. No doubt, she was most likely responding to my efforts, and not always to the content of what I had written.

Curiously, the pieces rarely changed much. Not much was altered, given that revising is something I do poorly and reluctantly. I liked what came out of my unconscious mind—without much pondering and planning because it seemed to come closest to the truth of what I was thinking and understanding—and alterations to that primary process of thinking seemed disruptive.

The essays are more or less psychological in nature. However, they are definitely not directed to a mental health readership; that is and never has been my wished-for audience. Instead, I am aiming to connect with intelligent, thoughtful, reflective individuals, all of whom are eager to think about these essays. I do not expect readers to always agree with my perspective, but I do expect them to at least be stimulated to think about and question what I have written.

I have always loved discourse; it was, hands down, the way I learned most easily. As a youngster I had a major reading inhibition, so I learned to listen and learn from conversation and dialogue between people. Thankfully, that inhibition eventually dissolved itself, opening an enormous world of literature and reading that was unavailable to me before then. But the love of discussion and interchange has never left me and is still the best way for me to learn and expand my infrastructure of knowledge and understanding.

This collection of essays that burst forth in a short period of time helped me pass the dreary days of COVID-19 (still not over as I write this) and kept my mind active and alert. I sincerely hope that these essays will also stimulate readers to ask hard questions and question ideas (even long-held ones) to see if they still make sense. My hope is that readers will allow themselves to be open to revision and updating if necessary. As I have said before, I do not profess to have the answers to the questions I have raised in these essays, and I am eager to hear what ideas may have been sparked in readers as a result. Through disparate perspectives we learn and expand our intellectual horizons. If that happens for the readers of this collection, my goal has been realized.

The title of this collection, *Life Lived in Small Moments*, revolves around a concept of particular importance to me. A relative often quoted an expression in his native language that, roughly translated, meant "life is made up of small moments." I believe he meant that we must embrace and cherish those everyday moments when we feel our aliveness and vitality. The huge moments in life—those of great acclaim, great success, or outstanding productivity—are few and far between. It's the little moments that occur every day—the ones in which we see ourselves in action and doing our own bidding—that make life vital, energized, and precious.

I have tried, in searching for common themes that may run through the essays, to delineate what I think are central concepts. It has not been an easy task: on the surface, the issues raised are often atypical topics and unusual viewpoints, and there will certainly be some readers who see the essays as trivial, superfluous, wrong-minded, or maybe even misguided, but if it stirs them to think about why they feel that way, and they are able to substantiate their points of view, my wishes for this book will have been fulfilled. I hope to stimulate new and creative thoughts in readers, as happened for me while writing.

Needless to say, I am deeply appreciative and thankful for the participation and involvement my wife, Julia, has had in these essays.

Without our evocative discussions, many of the essays would not have happened. I am often blinded and befuddled by her perspectives, but when I listen more intently and with heightened and open-minded curiosity, I am able to see her perspective, as well as her true insights. How lucky I am to have found a partner like her. I am truly happy that our discourse and discussions of any topic will never end, allowing for ever-increasing, ongoing intellectual growth, understanding, and insight.

Leonard D. Elkun, MD
Fall 2020

PART 1
DECAY OF THE EMPIRE

1

Aging in America, Part 1
Growing Old

I BELIEVE IT IS A RATHER sad state of affairs that the process of aging in America is seen in such negative terms.

While it is obviously true that we all age one day each day, the awareness of that process does not hit us until much later in life. And when it does, it can—if we are not careful and sensitive—give rise to a feeling of panic. The statement, "Time is running out and I have not achieved everything I was hoping for," is one possible effect of becoming aware of the passage of time, and the fact that our time on earth is limited.

But there may be an even deeper and more ominous awareness that occurs with the recognition that time is running out, or more simply put, *time is running*. I believe that underlying the more superficial sense—my body is not what it used to be, I move more slowly and seem to have less energy, I require more rest, I don't seem to have the motivation and interests I used to when younger—is a deeper sense that I must now face the recognition that I am not immortal. One day, I will not be here.

The magnitude of that awareness is monumental. Children certainly, and for an extended period of time, encompass the feeling that they will be here forever—it is probably important to have that feeling so as not to feel the pressure of time at that stage of life.

As age creeps up and the awareness that we will not be here forever becomes more evident, there is a need to come to terms with that evolving truism. It is a serious and deeply felt blow to our narcissism and sense of self to know our time is limited. The idea that the world will go on without us, and that we may even eventually be forgotten, is a devastating fact to have to deal with. Very few of us will have left such a critical contribution to the world that our being and presence on earth will be long remembered. Most of us will simply not have that pleasure.

The clear problem with the observation that we are not immortal and will not see how it all turns out for the world or for our family or friends is part of the potential panic we might feel as we acknowledge the aging process. And unfortunately here in the U.S., as well as other places in the world, the advance of technology guarantees a feeling of increasing obsolescence, in that what was new yesterday is old, replaceable, and fungible today.

Because that statement pertains to people as well, the aging process can leave us feeling old, useless, and of little value (in comparison to our younger selves), all of which adds to the sense that we are quickly passing through life and will not be here forever, as we had once wished. And there seems to be no respite or escape from that obvious truth. But is that the real truth? Is there no escape from that reality?

The answer is an existential one. Namely, that we must make each and every day be a day in which we seek and find pleasure, and find ways to stimulate our minds and bodies, by which I mean pleasure and satisfaction of all kinds and in all spheres of our lives. I do not mean to imply that we must become hedonistic and seek and find "out-of-the-ordinary" pleasures, but rather to keep a focus on the daily ability to find richness in activities of all kinds, be it physical or intellectual, interactive or in isolation, productive or non-productive. The critical characteristic is that it brings satisfaction and the feeling that life is worth living. The aging process will often afford us time and opportunity to explore a wide range of options for seeking pleasure, in that we are free to try new activities, take on new challenges, and hopefully escape the rat race we experienced in our younger years. The more we see aging as an opportunity to be stimulated and generous, spread wisdom, learn new things, and try anything, the less we will feel the pain of that loss of immortality. The concept of the transformation of individual narcissism into a sense of "cosmic" narcissism is particularly relevant in this process of overcoming the narcissistic assault of eventual death for all of us. While we may not live on indefinitely, the world and the people we care about will be around after us (at least for a while), so the idea that we have abandoned personal narcissism, at least for the most part, can be comforting.

During a visit to Southeast Asia, it appeared to me that the aging process had a vastly different flavor than in the U.S. While old is still old, people seem to have adopted a very different view of aging and the elderly. Rather than becoming obsolete, useless, and sent out to pasture, there is a palpable respect and admiration for older folks, and a rather dramatic and obvious inclusion of them into the daily life of families and society. For example, in observing the manner in which younger monks relate to the older (and far more experienced and knowledgeable) monks, one can easily see that there is a feeling of usefulness and value given to the wisdom, experience, and worldliness of the older monks. And rather than putting them out to pasture, they are a central and meaningful part of family and society, and their perspectives are welcomed. They are not banished to the backwaters, as is the case too often in Western cultures, especially the U.S. As such, they are given the opportunities to remain active, important, respected, admired, and valuable to their communities. As a result, they may avoid the pain of aging in an environment where you are not valued or sought out, or your perspectives encouraged.

Perhaps it is also the Buddhist philosophy (religion?) that helps with this favorable transition into aging in that culture. There is a constant striving to find a place of peace, harmony, and inner tranquility—the concept seems to be that the older we get, the more practiced and efficient we are at finding that inner space of peace and mindfulness. Aging provides us with the pathway, through experience, wisdom, and reflection, to find that inner space of harmony with the world around us and with one another, and most importantly with ourselves. Rather than becoming useless and obsolete as we age, the elderly (practitioners of Buddhism) are getting closer to a state of Nirvana, the sought-after place of Buddhism, via their experience, practice, and understanding of what is most critical and valuable in life, namely the discovery and enjoyment of inner peace. Sadly, that concept in Western cultures may be seen as too soft and easygoing, and totally out of step with our hard-driving and power-hungry society. It's a rather sad statement and suggestion of who we have become, and what we look forward to, as we age in our Western culture and society.

But as is the case in all situations, we need not follow the masses: each of us is truly free to choose how we live, in both our younger and older ages. We can chart our own pathways and direct our energies and interests however we feel internally motivated to do so. And while we may not seek the very particular Nirvana of Buddhism, we are free to seek our own, idiosyncratically designed "heaven on earth," one full of our own unique wishes and dreams. And we are utterly free to bring all our energies and drive to satisfying ourselves however we may choose, at the expense of becoming less valuable and relevant as we age. Are we compelled to accept that premise? I think not.

2

Aging in America, Part 2
Approaching Eighty

I N AUGUST 2020, I CELEBRATED my eightieth birthday. And while I have addressed this issue before, I have certainly thought about it many more times recently.

Of course, I appreciate the significance of reaching that ripe old age, and what it means for most of us. Certainly, at a much earlier time in life, to be eighty years of age seemed like a million years away. The appreciation for time and the passage of time were barely noticeable, and not worthy of much note. Time was endless, and the end of time for each of us at that early stage of life was an almost impossible outcome. It wasn't that we did not intellectually understand that life ends for all of us, but rather that it is one of the hardest things to address directly—namely that one day we will no longer be here.

To encompass that idea emotionally in my twenties, thirties, and even forties was a difficult thing to grasp, and especially to address directly. It was difficult because my response at the time was that it didn't really impact me because I was still young and had infinite time left on earth. In fact, I even felt that I wasn't sure I would ever be gone. Why couldn't immortality be mine?

But time inevitably marches on, and the dawning awareness of that passage begins to strike us, albeit at different times for each of us. We can become aware of it earlier, for example, with the onset of a serious disease, the loss of someone close to us, or by watching others around us who seem to be aging and changing as time goes by. We may notice that time seems to be clumped together as we age: it may become hard to differentiate what happened at my thirty-fifth birthday party, my forty-sixth Christmas party, or when I took that trip to France—whatever grouping of particular memories. The subtle distinction of time becomes somewhat blurred. It does not represent the early onset of Alzheimer's, but instead reflects that our minds are filled with many memories and many bits of information, the distinction of which (in time) may not matter all that much.

It is also true that history has a distinct way of revising itself over time, thus the necessity to connect to those old times and old memories and experiences becomes a bit less relevant, especially if you know the recollections may not be an accurate replay of what realistically occurred. It is interesting to speculate the ways in which memories revise themselves. Are the painful aspects of the experience dampened, or intensified? Are the joyous aspects made more powerful, or less profound? Are the revisions so that self-esteem can be preserved and enhanced, resulting in the holder of the memory feeling less guilty, ashamed, or embarrassed? The likely answer is that the revisions will usually release the memory-holder from the more negative aspects of that specific memory, whatever they may be.

The aging process and people's reactions to it are the source of many questions.

There is, of course, the age-old question of the meaning of life. Why have we been put on this earth? Is there an explanation, and is it necessary to explain that question in order to make life worthwhile? And what is the purpose of living, another typical question, but one different from the question of meaning. These questions have been debated forever. The whole issue of heaven, a life-after-death event, or a place to land is another typical and frequent question that comes up with the aging process. And while there are no definitive answers to these critical questions, they seem to come up as we age and anticipate death and dying.

How often do we hear the idea of "a life well lived," especially when we discuss a person's life after they have departed? We usually assume the phrase is symbolic for a person who has lived a life of gratification, joy, and substance. And those existentialists amongst us will say that the life lived today is where the focus needs to be, and the future be damned, because I cannot know what comes next. But what I do know is that I will chase fun and satisfaction today, because I cannot focus on yesterday (which is gone), or on tomorrow, which is not yet here.

There is the common idea that life is made up of small moments of joy and pleasure, and that to wait for those great moments of admiration or satisfaction that come so infrequently may result in the waste of a lifetime.

The question arises, "What is the reason that we hang on to life so definitively and tenaciously, even at the last moment, when it is natural to let go?" Even the person with a serious and painful terminal illness is rarely eager to give up on life, even if he knows that an escape from his suffering awaits. Life is precious, and the time we have is guarded like the most valuable treasure we own. We are so reluctant to waste that commodity, a product that we cannot replace nor do over again.

As one reaches eighty years, and life seems to be drawing down, how do we feel about it, and what do we do to take advantage of the time we have? I can unequivocally say that there is absolutely no reason to panic about the utilization of time left. The focus needs to be on making it valuable and joyful. Since we rarely, if ever, know when that fateful day will come, to worry about that date is a total waste of time and energy. The only reasonable choice is to live heartily—like the common expression goes, "Live your life today like it is your last day on earth." Unfortunately, too many people are unable to utilize the time they do have. They are bogged down with a variety of distracting concerns. What will my legacy be? Will I leave enough financial support for my family, so that they can go on admiring my successes? How will I be remembered, and for what? How long will my name cross peoples' lips once I'm gone?

Clearly, these concerns take one away from the task at hand. The task, and perhaps the only task, is to actively and aggressively use your time wisely and creatively, and to make the most of the opportunities and options that you do have. Stay connected with those people that have been the most meaningful and valuable to you in your life. And it is wise to focus on the small moments and give up on waiting for the big score and big moments which come so terribly rarely anyway.

So, in approaching eighty years of age, the lesson of greatest significance to be learned is that time is precious, and how you choose to use it is entirely up to you. There are no restrictions to what you can do or try to do. It is critical not to be distracted from the task, by focusing and diverting your attention on what you think you ought to do, or what others may expect of you. And it behooves you to be experimental and pursue your dreams, even if they are seemingly out of the ordinary for you. No one is there to judge you, and neither should you be judgmental of your own decisions. Approaching eighty years of age has been a really interesting transition. I have realized that if I keep my eyes on the singular goal of pursuing pleasure and fun, within reason, it will happen and make the last years fruitful and joyous, no matter the length of time I have left. As stated earlier, since we never know when our time is up, why not live today like it's our last day?

3

Aging in America, Part 3
What Goes Around

DURING THE CORONAVIRUS CRISIS, MY wife and I take one- to two-hour walks each day to get exercise (gyms were closed), but also to get out of the house to remember that a world exists outside of the four walls of our home. During one of our walks we discussed the way in which assisted living facilities were being utterly ravaged by the virus, and the elderly (especially ones with any kind of compromised immune system) were dying in huge droves.

Our observations stimulated a discussion of why people are in assisted living facilities in such large numbers. My wife comes from Europe, where the idea of old folks being placed in assisted living facilities is seen strictly as a last resort, and only when the management of an elder at home becomes an impossibility. She knows that I used to consult for nursing homes for many years and that I have a lot of firsthand knowledge of these settings. A serious discussion ensued between us as to why there seems to be so many more elderly persons in these facilities in America.

We also discussed how easily mothers in America can utilize day care facilities for baby care and how they do not have other options but to have their child or children spend eight to ten hours per workday in a day care facility. Needless to say, it is a significant expense. Even while they may lament that their children are being raised by other (often changing) parental figures, they have no choice but to accept their choices if they are to continue to work and have any kind of comfortable existence.

My wife then made a not-so-funny comment: many people begin their early lives in day care facilities for children, and then as adults those same children may place their own aging parents or relatives in day care facilities for the elderly. One day those children may themselves be placed in day care facilities, continuing the cycle.

While this presented some dark humor the profundity of the comment struck home. It was the ultimate reciprocity between the children who grew up in day care facilities and went on to reciprocate by placing their own parents into day care.

For my European wife, the idea of the elderly being placed into nursing homes or assisted living facilities for almost any reason is seen and felt as a shameful act, and one that an individual would avoid at all costs. Taking care of aged parents, even parents who were incapacitated in some way at a later stage of life, is seen as a generous and important way to reciprocate the care that you received as a child from those very same, now elderly, parents. It raised the obvious question of why it is seemingly so easy to have an elderly person placed in one of those facilities.

I have seen in my experience consulting to those settings that many people are admitted because the children or grandchildren simply cannot—or do not want to—take care of those older, more needy individuals. The reasons for admission are not always so crystal clear, and all too often you get the sense that the elderly are being dumped into the assisted living system because it is too much trouble to care for them at home. I realize that certain older persons—especially those with serious illnesses such as Alzheimer's, advanced heart or pulmonary diseases, or difficult physical problems—may need more specialized and intensive care and supervision, but that is not always the case when patients are admitted to these facilities. So, what makes it so much easier here in America to put the elderly "away," when in other countries, like those in Europe or Asia, it is far less frequent or acceptable?

Is there something about our society that lends itself to that ease of abandoning the elderly to these settings? To be sure, the separation of families and disintegration of the family compound concept (the idea of wanting to live in the same community as your parents and grandparents) has lost its cache and appeal. We now tend to live far away from our older family members, and while this is not a ubiquitous phenomenon, there is far less a feeling of responsibility for these relatives, and more a sense of burden that we are now responsible for their care and it dramatically interferes with our day-to-day lives. It is not so hard to see how, with distance and a resultant lack of connection and feeling of responsibility, that it would be easier to admit that elderly sick relative than keep them at home, thereby increasing your burden enormously.

Another issue is the relative lack of respect for the aged and the wisdom they have acquired over time. Do people still want to hear what Grandfather or Grandmother have to say? Do they want to hear their stories of the good old days? In far too many cases, the answer is no. In this new technological age, old is useless and what is new becomes old tomorrow. What can Grandfather or Grandmother really have to offer our modern world? In our current ultra-utilitarian society, they are seen as outdated and out of sync. And it is true that maybe elders do not know the latest technology and the latest video games, nor do they buy into social media hype, but those who have been around and experienced a lot of the transitions and changes over time have gained wisdom for the travails of daily life. Unfortunately, if there is little interest in the wisdom of the ages, then the informed information and knowledge that comes through the processing of experience has no fertile place to land.

But perhaps the most relevant and powerful motive for the marginalization of the elderly in today's American society is the advent of the "me first" philosophy. The currently honored concept of taking care of oneself first is a leading motivation for people in our society. There seems to be little room or even time for generosity or caring for others. While we do have exemplary philanthropic role models, such as Bill and Melinda Gates, Warren Buffet, and many others, what they donate is money and not necessarily caring and concern for others on a direct basis. Donating money to worthwhile causes does help and is obviously important, but we also need to personally support individuals in need, especially elders. Unfortunately, those direct and intimate contacts are often lower on the priority list. If one accepts the premise of "me first," and lives by that premise regularly, it is not hard to see why the rates of admissions to assisted living facilities and nursing homes are on the rise in our modern society.

In fact, there may even be a slight criticism of those individuals who might choose to keep their elderly at home and care for them as best they can—they are seen as being cheap, avoiding work (outside the home), or even as part of a subterranean plan to extract money from the elderly. Rather than that choice being seen as an act of generosity and caring, and true reciprocity to those who cared for us earlier in life— and because it is a choice made less and less—there exists the need to rationalize and justify the choices we have made in not caring for our elders. Instead, it is much easier to choose a comfortable assisted living facility, place our elders there, and go on about our own business.

The lack of care and support for the elderly comes through in many ways. At the present time, but not limited to the current pandemic situation at the time of this essay (which will one day pass), it has been obvious that interest and care-giving for that population has been woefully negligent. The death rate amongst that group is much higher than it needs to be. While it is certainly true that the elderly are far more vulnerable and likely to be stricken with all kinds of illness due to diminished immunological vitality, the numbers of deaths are still higher than they ought to be if more care and attention were paid to them. They are seen as fungible and expendable, and not as the mothers, fathers, grandmothers, and grandfathers who brought us into this world, changed our diapers, fed us, and told us nighttime stories before bed.

We tend to forget that the elderly are still people who have emotional lives, and who feel and react. And so, how seriously do we consider how that person reacts internally when they find themselves placed into a nursing home or assisted living facility, especially if it is not because of their choice, and may even be against their wishes? It is hard enough to end up feeling abandoned and left to die in one of those institutions, but the awareness that the efforts you have made over your lifetime to contribute to your family and friends have not earned you the right to remain at home, when possible, and that you have been casually "dropped" into this new setting to fend for yourself makes it unbearable. These feelings may also mirror those of the young child when he is dropped off at the day care facility because Mom and Dad have to go to work. The child may wonder if they will ever come back to pick him up, or if he has been abandoned. The elder left at the old-age facility to fend for himself, not knowing if and when he will receive a visit from a relative or friend, may experience those same emotions.

This is the height of irony and reciprocity.

4

The End of Civilization in America, Part 1
Vicissitudes

MY WIFE AND I HAVE had the good fortune of having traveled to several countries. In November 2018 we spent ten days in Italy (primarily in Rome). In March 2019 we spent one week in Fiji and then three weeks in Australia. In August 2019 we returned from an eleven-day excursion to Serbia. In September of that same year we traveled to Thailand, Cambodia, and Vietnam. What stood out to us in each of the countries and cultures we visited was the kind of civility and welcome we encountered. When I wrote this essay, we hadn't yet traveled to Southeast Asia, but our experience was the same.

Italians are well known for their hospitality and openheartedness, and our experience reflected that. Almost without exception the Italians we encountered were willing to communicate and share ideas and were open to people of different backgrounds. This was true regardless of whether someone was affluent. There's a reason you rarely hear of people returning from a trip to Italy complaining about the lack of receptivity or helpfulness amongst the Italian natives.

In Fiji it was even more dramatic, where the degree of civility and open-mindedness exhibited by the Fijians seemed infinite. They were only too willing to be helpful, instructive, and genuinely concerned about our experiences on their island. This was true of almost every individual we came across: we did not see any evidence whatsoever of envy, greed, jealousy, or animosity towards foreigners (like ourselves) even though resentment would have been understandable because most, if not all, of the locals could not afford to pay the exorbitant prices for hotels and meals that we were able to enjoy.

In Australia, we stayed with locals for three weeks—we considered our hosts newly-found friends. While it is true that the two individuals we visited were unique in their capacity for generosity and willingness to interact and engage at the deepest levels, to host people you hardly know for three weeks exemplifies a kind of civility, gentleness, and concern for other human beings. To us, it (and they) seemed quite exceptional. But we also met with *their* friends and relatives who also showed that kind of willingness to accept strangers into their lives and homes—all without any sign of animosity or competitiveness.

When we visited Serbia the totality of the "welcome home" feelings that people expressed and extended to us was beyond our wildest expectations. I do not know how we could have been made more comfortable, or felt more curiosity extended in our direction, especially given that Julia, my wife, had not been home for twenty-nine years. These people wanted to know who we really were. Julia's family—including her extended—traveled to see us and tried everything within their power to make us feel comfortable, including showering us with meaningful gifts. Their generosity and willingness to take on new connections was immediate and intensely profound and filled with honesty and authenticity.

So, what is this capacity for civility and willingness to help others; the concern for the well-being of one's "brothers" and "sisters"? Is it some genetic trait that is transmitted from generation to generation, or is it related to earlier experiences in life that leads one to feel that kind of openheartedness and willingness to interact in a civil way? A plausible definition of civilization is to think of a community in general, one where there exists an attitude of sharing and of mutual concern for the well-being of others: as a member of that society, one can add certain characteristics that will facilitate a sense of unity and comfort. The assumption is that others will do similarly, creating an environment of cooperation and expanding comfort and ease for all. If I share vegetables from my garden with you, and you share some from your garden with me, we will both be far better off and have that much more variety to choose from. The ability to provide that for each other yields pleasure and enhanced self-esteem to the "givers" from both sides of the fence. That is a civilized society.

It is probably accurate to suggest that an early experience in which one is taken care of, and handled with empathy, is far more likely to lead to a civilized individual, one who is willing to provide for others, because he knows what it feels like to be taken care of. But when one's early experiences have been those of deprivation or starvation, and lack of affection or empathy, that individual is far less likely to be willing or able to provide for his fellow man. In that case, he is too needy within himself to share his "vegetables." He needs all of them for himself, or at least feels that way. "Why should I provide for you? You take care of yourself, and I'll take care of myself." That response is not an attitude that leads to mutual concern, sharing, or a sense of a "civilized" community. "Every man for himself" is the not-so-buried attitude of an uncivilized community.

How generous we are to others, and how we might experience a rise in good feeling by giving to our brothers, is reflected in our children—they will likely adopt that same value system. And to the extent that we are enriched and enhanced in good feelings by giving to others and being available to support, love, and honor others will also be incorporated by the next generation. If children witness an envious, fiercely competitive parent, one who cannot celebrate someone else's success or feels the need to take down his fellow man at every opportunity, what then can we expect of those children who witness that on a daily basis?

It is naïve to expect that child to be able to give to others without reservation. He will feel put upon, taken advantage of, and at times obliged to give and support his fellow man, but it will never flow easily and with honesty, and will never yield heightened self-esteem.

In America today, I believe we are living in a land with disintegrating civility and a civilization that is rotting at its very core. We do not have an attitude of generosity. Instead, we are far too narcissistically driven, even admired and celebrated for our self-centered behaviors. And to be generous in the way I described above in other countries and cultures is to be laughed at, and seen as a sucker or a foil. Perhaps this is not true in every community and in every household, but it is far too prevalent. We are led by leaders who admire self-centeredness and egotistical behavior and take joy and pride in tearing down the self-esteem of others, especially those who might oppose them.

What kind of civilization is it that caters to bearers of arms, despite repeated and increasingly frequent violent crimes, homicides, and suicides, the destruction of temples, mosques, and churches? There are no places that are totally safe these days from some lunatic, gun-toting cowboy, who feels it is acceptable to shoot people—in fact, he may even consider it his right, because he knows he will be supported by high-powered organizations that protect and preserve the right to bear arms. In fact, in America it is becoming even more necessary to protect yourself from these lunatics who feel empowered by a leadership that encourages violence and protects nationalistic groups and right-wing fanatical organizations. Where is the outraged public that says we cannot have our children and citizens shot at just because someone is angry, hurt, or wants to get even? Why have we not risen up against this home-grown terrorism, far more powerful and destructive than any outside our borders? I posit that the answer is, we have lost our civility and our feeling of protecting and standing up for our neighbors—behaviors that are seen as the stuff of weaklings and "lefties," and the way-too-soft citizens of our country. Rather than being seen as courageous and standing up for what is right and full of integrity, these behaviors are seen as the exact opposite.

Does this all represent a disintegration of civilization as we have known it, or as we have experienced in other cultures and countries? I believe what is happening is powerfully symbolic of what is wrong and foul smelling in this country. And the real tragedy is that no one will stand up and say so. How have we failed our citizenry and managed to create such awful examples to show our children? What can we expect going forward if this disintegration and degradation continues? More violence, more disregard for the violence, and a perpetration and facilitation of further uncivilized, undisciplined, and destructive behaviors.

Is this the legacy we leave our children and our children's children? My fear is that this pattern will not be interrupted, and we will continue to have leadership that encourages violence and preaches disrespect for others, particularly if others are opposing in their opinions. Rather than seeing value in debate, and encouraging learning and acquisition of wisdom from discussing opposing ideas, there will be death-yielding rewards for holding divergent opinions. Either you are in, or you are a dead man.

How have other countries and cultures maintained a willingness to be generous and giving to their tribal members, and even to non-tribal members? It is a valued part of their culture to be open and accepting of your brother, and the issue of family integrity and sharing has been perpetuated over the centuries. But in America, we see that behavior as being too dependent on family and instead encourage distance and separation, so that every man stands on his own and must be an independent nation, one in which your goal is to be sure your neighbor does not steal your vegetables. This paranoia is part of and symbolic of the inevitable disintegration and loss of a civilized society. Is it a reversible condition? Probably not as long as narcissism and self-indulgence reign supreme. As long as we have leadership that encourages violent behavior—with perhaps the best example of that being the enormity and reemergence of racism—and defends that behavior, things will not change in any significant way.

As long as disrespect is admired and violence is facilitated—as long as leadership turns a blind or an ignorant eye towards this disintegration—we can only expect things to get worse. One has only to study the fall of the Roman and Greek Empires to see the pattern of slow and steady deterioration of civilized behavior. And now, America the Great is following suit.

5

The End of Civilization in America, Part 2
And Justice for All?

IN READING PLATO'S *REPUBLIC* WE see a whole text devoted to a subtle and yet profound definition of justice and how it plays out in ancient society. The question arises: does justice have a different meaning and expression in modern times as compared to times long past? Justice implies a kind of balanced and fair-minded approach to the rules of law. These are rules that govern human interaction and man's dealing with his fellow man, as well as civilization. These rules attempt to regulate and modulate man's dealing with others, so that life can exist and proceed in a civilized manner. There exists certain rewards for following and abiding by the rules, and punishment for disobeying or defying them. Prejudice and political motives should never affect the outcome of legitimate dispute. Justice implies that neutral parties will evaluate (judge) the facts as presented and make decisions based upon the rule of law. Preference and advantage should not be a part of just decisions. And yet, if we carefully evaluate current renditions of justice in our present-day judicial system, does neutrality exist? Are unbiased decisions the rule or the exception? It appears that in today's court system there are many extraneous and perhaps unwelcome factors that influence decision-making. Neutral evaluation of the facts and non-biased decisions are more and more the exception.

The judicial system and the practitioners within are under enormous pressure at times to come up with decisions and findings that are not based upon a neutral exploration of the facts in a legal matter. Instead, they are more likely to be politically motivated, yielding advantage (often undeserved) to one party or the other. And is it always intentional manipulation of facts that leads an evaluator to faulty decision-making— or is it that the evaluator (judge) simply does not understand the critical elements in a legal matter, refuses to acknowledge certain factors, or does not do the necessary homework in adjudicating a matter? All are possible, but the most repulsive option is choosing to ignore certain factors, or interpreting the presented material to please or satisfy some external force that has brought pressure to the evaluator for a variety of reasons. Because judges and evaluators have enormous latitude in their decision-making, it is often impossible to determine the avenues they followed to make those decisions. It is true that there are ways of challenging judges' decisions, but these ways are arduous, and often seen as provocative and even disrespectful. They are generally not encouraged, and in fact are probably actively discouraged, leaving people on the short end of their decisions in extremely difficult positions. To challenge a decision is costly, time-consuming, and goes directly against the mainstream of current day justice.

We are led by individuals in federal, state, and local governments who seem to make up their own rules and, when a particular rule does not suit their fancy, either ignore it, override it, or certainly disregard it. If you are caught with your hand in the cookie jar, simply deny it vehemently. The idea is that if you stick to your story, making up excuses and lies to substantiate your idea and your position, eventually your story will be believed, or your accusers will relent. The liar that believes his own lies can be a very forceful opponent, even in a court of law. It is not uncommon to see lawyers and counselors having the equivalent of a temper tantrum in the courtroom, and in an effort to preserve decorum, judges yielding to their demands and allegations, rather than standing up for justice. Judges also want to be liked and respected, and they will bend and twist to get the recognition they feel they deserve, even at the expense of delivering justice.

All too often in American courts, the blustering, vociferous, accusing lawyer will get his way, and the victim of that rant is rendered powerless to defend against that rant. Like others, judges require courage and fortitude and a strong sense of confidence to enable them to challenge and confront false accusations and blustering attorneys acting up in front of them. It is simply easier for them to acquiesce at times, rather than stand up for justice.

In America, judgeships and appointments to the court system are largely by appointment, and even those who are elected after being supported by the more powerful of the parties in a particular district or county system. Appointments are not always contingent on qualifications, but rather on who you know, who is sponsoring you, and how influential and powerful your sponsor is. All too often, we see judges appointed to the court system who get there by behind-the-scenes activity, instead of competence. In such a system how can one reasonably expect justice and fairness, when the judge sitting in a position of making critical decisions has gotten there through "under the table" means? It is naïve to think that a case's outcome will not be subject to undue influence coming from some exterior source and quite separate from the facts.

The system appears to be broken, does not respond to the needs of the average person, and is under tremendous influence from outside sources and pressures—how can we understand this phenomenon? Is it a reflection of who we are as a country and as a society? I believe so; this system of justice clearly reflects the breakdown of our civilized and just society. To be fair-minded is no longer admired or respected. Instead, to confront the law, and challenge it at every turn, is "de rigueur." We have leaders and their compadres who see themselves operating far above the law, and not constrained by the usual rules of decency or being respectful of the rule of law. In fact, they laugh in the face of rules and constraints, and go about their business of doing whatever pleases and satisfies their decadent and perverse needs.

And so, this is the example for the nation. How can we then be surprised to see the corruption and dishonesty pervade through all the systems of government and society? For the rule of law to be seen as antiquated and outdated, and perhaps even laughable? If those legal rules and regulations stand in the way, simply disregard them, and go about your business no matter what you have to do to accomplish your goals, and forget any adherence to the ordinary rules that the ordinary men must abide by! That brand of thinking, self-aggrandizing, and out-of-control thinking is at the root of our broken judicial system. To fix it is a major concern and problem for the average man, who is still subject to those rules. Is it a surprise that we feel helpless, not listened to, and impotent?

6

The End of Civilization in America, Part 3
Pride

NATIONAL PRIDE WAS SOMETHING THAT, as Americans, we were always happy to have as part of our lives. Pride in the nation you live in seems natural; something that every citizen, in any country, will have a sense of. National pride should be a feeling that warms the heart and gives you a sense of poignancy. For many years Americans have felt an enormous sense of pride in our country, based upon a wide array of attributes and factors. America has always been recognized as a "melting pot" where individuals of all colors, creeds and religions were made to feel welcome and at home. For many decades this idea was embraced and something we all felt good about. We took enormous pride in our generosity of spirit and empathy for those who have suffered. We felt good knowing we were the most powerful, industrious, creative, and wealthy nation on the planet. We enjoyed the respect of most, if not all, of the nations of the world, and were seen as indisputable leaders and protectors of peace across the globe. Nations turned to us for help, leadership, and direction, because we had shown ourselves to be competent, prepared, productive, and efficient in the endeavors we undertook. And we made ourselves available to others in need.

As I write this (in 2020), I find myself asking, what has happened? America has lost its position of respect, admiration, and preference. Instead, it has become a source of serious pain and shame. It can be hard to understand why the nation has dissipated so rapidly over these past few years, but it is clearly related to the functioning of our federal government and its obvious and utter lack of empathy and understanding of individual suffering and pain. This lack of empathy, coupled with an overt and profound preoccupation with the acquisition of power, money, and status has eroded the very fabric of this once-powerful nation. It is somewhat baffling that a reputation won over many decades and even centuries could evaporate so quickly. The change in the basic nature of our government and its clear and unpopular priorities has contributed to that disintegration.

It has become hard to even admit to being an American these days, or to be proud of our country. Even though individually we are not responsible for the country's loss of the reputation and respect, it is a tremendous source of personal shame and embarrassment: we still feel the pain. That pain can be compared to the pride we take in our home team winning the Super Bowl or the World Series, or the sadness when they lose. As we experience the deterioration of respect and positive regard for our homeland, we feel that loss personally, even if that loss was beyond our control.

Pride is based on a realistic assessment of the effective functioning of a person, city, or country. When that person or place is not functioning in effective and empathic ways, especially when dealing with other human beings, embracing that feeling of pride becomes increasingly difficult, if not impossible. While it does not necessarily interfere with our day-to-day lives, the loss of pride does leave us sad and even bitter. And what makes it far worse is that we are totally impotent to change what is clearly happening to this country.

We can divide pride into primary and secondary pride. Pride in one's country, favorite team, even a child's success, are all examples of secondary pride—it is derived by external events and stimuli. We may not be directly involved in the events that lead to the feeling. Primary pride is a far more important source of self-esteem and positive internal feeling, and is derived from aspects of one's own direct involvement and participation—graduating from college, starting your own business, finishing your first marathon, having your first child. What is most relevant is your direct involvement in events that yield the feeling of pride, and that the experience is internally motivated. Primary pride is often related to the achievement of privately held and internally established goals and aims within your psyche.

When we return to the issue of the death of nationalistic pride, we discover that what would ordinarily yield prideful feelings for the nation is now a source of inordinate shame and embarrassment. When we witness on a regular basis evidence of a leadership that lies, confabulates stories of convenience, exaggerates, begs for admiration, passes misinformation, practices nepotism boldly and bare-faced, and is clearly xenophobic, racist, and not empathic, how is it possible to feel any kind of pride in the nation? Pride has been increasingly buried in a deep hole, and has died a painful and shameful death, based upon the criteria listed above.

Can it be turned around? While the current leadership continues its malignant, destructive, and infinitely selfish ways, restored prideful behavior remains a distant possibility. But since hope is the last emotion to die, there is indeed hope for the future. The current leadership, despite its attitudes and wishes, is not a monarchy or dictatorship, so its time will also pass. The sooner there is a united and active move against the current state of affairs, including the current leadership, done in an appropriate and responsible manner, we will move on and find ways to regain our pride. America will once again be known for its empathy, justice, generosity, and openness to foreigners.

While it is incredible to think how quickly the pride of this nation died its painful death, it may also portend a rapid recovery. Each of us, in our own way, must attempt to unearth and dig up that buried pride, beginning with ourselves. We must find within ourselves love for our fellow man, without prejudice, without xenophobia, without racism, and without harsh judgment of the inevitable differences amongst ourselves. A working "melting pot" benefits everybody, not just the privileged few.

7

The End of Civilization in America, Part 4
Who Gets to Die First?

THERE IS A VERY INTERESTING phenomenon taking place during the 2020 COVID-19 pandemic regarding the reopening of the economy in the U.S. Clearly, there is a major divide amongst the population. Some are eager to continue to "shelter in place" to protect one another from infection. It has been a mostly successful way to attack this invisible enemy, which essentially eludes the usual understanding our scientists have on epidemic activity. Others are eager to forgo sheltering in order to resume life as we knew pre-COVID. This latter group has a variety of motives for wanting to resume that life, some health-related and some not. The thrust of those who would keep us on lockdown until we have the virus under control are correct in that you first have to attend adequately to containing the virus. The argument against this is that those people are not considering the issue of an economy that is breaking down, if not already broken: it will take a long, painful time to recover from the damage.

Those who want a more rapid reopening are motivated in many ways, some of which are perfectly understandable and reasonable. For example, even with additional support from the government in the form of extra unemployment compensation, the millions of people laid off or furloughed from work are anxious to get back to earning a living (without federal assistance). This group is caught between a rock and a hard place. They need to generate income, but also want to protect their families from sickness and poverty. This group of workers—lower- and even middle-income—have very hard decisions to make and are not in enviable positions. Either choice—staying home or going back to work—carries great potential dangers and hardships for them.

For the most part, white collar workers have the option to work from home. Their danger levels are far less dramatic and poignant than the group mentioned above. Of course, they can still become infected, but they have options that can more effectively protect them and their families.

Then there is the group that wants to reopen things because they object to being told what to do and perceive that they are having their civil rights infringed on. This appears to be especially true for younger people, who either feel or were told they are far less vulnerable to the virus. Many of them feel it's acceptable for the elderly and sick to not be able to move about freely and exercise those same rights, because of their obvious susceptibility to illness. But why should anyone else be restricted? There is also the belligerent, angry, gun-toting group that doesn't seem to be concerned about exposing themselves—or others— to the virus.

Lastly, we have the corporate elites: the owners, bosses, and CEOs of large companies who have every conceivable option available to them. It is obvious why they want a rapid reopening of this country: how else will their large corporations and companies make money? These corporations and companies can adapt and manage. Frankly, it does not appear that this group is either in touch with the dangers that the other groups are exposed to, or what the impact might be on them or their families. If they are concerned, they do not appear to care, notice, or be bothered by it. What is most important is the acquisition of money and power.

To corporate elites and some politicians, the exposure of lower-income workers is part of the price of being an American, except that it does absolutely not pertain to them. To die for your country, in order to save the precious economy, should, in fact, be an honorable act. Never mind the impact or disruption to some poor worker's life. In fact, there was a young congressman from Indiana, not very slick or sophisticated in my opinion, who suggested people of a certain age (I think it was seventy) should be willing to sacrifice themselves to save the economy of our country. The idea is preposterous, but it makes you wonder how widespread it is. To have even proposed that idea reveals the insensitivity of certain legislators in America. He is undoubtedly not alone in this thought.

While it is certainly a serious issue that our economy is in trouble, at what cost do we try to resurrect it? Does the death of a few hundred thousand Americans pay that price? Much like Nazi Germany in the 1930s and 1940s, do we accept that the elderly and the vulnerable are expendable? During WWII, the Nazi party considered people as dispensable and fungible, especially if they were considered less than perfect. Here in America, minorities and workers on the front lines of the workforce are also considered disposable. How relevant is the life of a dishwasher at a local restaurant, or the garbage collector, or the landscape worker, to those higher up? It's easy to conclude that there is no serious concern or even awareness of the dangers they are being exposed to.

Thankfully, there are voices in the media and in local governments that seem to be very in tune with the dilemma. For example, the governors in a number of states have risen to the occasion and have presented a rational and sensible approach to dealing with the pandemic. In the absence of any true leadership at the federal level that is genuinely concerned, these individuals have stepped up and offered direction and solutions that make sense.

What does this rampant insensitivity represent about our country? How could we embrace a leadership that reeks of this kind of hostility and violence against others? Unfortunately, it is a testament to what this country has become. The concern for our fellow man is almost nonexistent, especially if it means having to sacrifice one's own existence to take care of another. Even for rational individuals, it is a hard decision to make. Should you go out once businesses and other facilities reopen? The issue of premature opening, based upon economic concerns, presents a major problem for many people. Most individuals will be very resistant and reluctant to resume going out into the public, even when they can.

Unfortunately, there is a huge percentage of the population who will not have the opportunity to make choices that make the most sense to them. The urgency to return to work, because of financial stresses, will blunt their judgment. Individuals that return to work because they have no other choice have a high chance of becoming infected and bringing the virus home to infect or even kill their families. It is beyond belief that certain well-known politicians and former politicians are able, with a straight face and seemingly without any sense of remorse or apprehension, to expect and encourage the return to the workplace so we can save the economy. The rationalization presented is that if we do not get people back to work and open up the economy, it will take years to restore life and the American economy to what it was pre-COVID. The fact that millions of individuals will be unnecessarily exposed to viral infections and death is irrelevant. So, what if we sacrifice another one hundred thousand people, or even more, to save our "way of life"? Can you realistically imagine anywhere else in the world where governmental leaders would openly say, "If people die to save our country, that's OK, and they should be proud to do so"? We shall see how many individuals close to these "leaders" are sacrificed, and how many of their family members and friends are volunteered for death. You can be absolutely assured that not even one will offer or put themselves in any danger. Perhaps hypocrisy, deceit, and greed are the true and everlasting signs of the current American way of life. Do we need to preserve those attributes by people dying at will?

8

Real Family Values

W E WERE LED TO BELIEVE that living in America was a
real gift: a land flowing with liberties and limitless opportunities where
you were free to pursue your dreams—and most likely achieve them. But
how true is that today? Is this still the land of opportunity and freedom?
It seems much more like a land of stress, complete with untold poverty,
where more than 90 percent of us lack even one thousand dollars in
emergency reserves. More than 55 percent of marriages end up in
divorce, and families feel more fractured and disrupted than ever before.
A college degree no longer guarantees economic security. In fact, about
half of college graduates report that six months after graduation they
cannot find acceptable employment that utilizes their college education.

Thus, it is hard to see the United States as a land "flowing with
milk and honey" or one that harbors the dreams and hopes of people
regardless of whether they are immigrants or native-born. In fact, more
and more, there is disappointment, disillusionment, and frustration.
Doing the "right thing" no longer seems to pay off—in fact, what does
pay off is far less clear. The old adage that hard work will bring success

seems harder and harder to embrace. So, where is the "joie de vivre" in America today? We seem so much more frustrated, even angry, with our place on the global stage, our politics, the lack of civilized feelings for one another—all overrun with unbridled narcissism and egotistical behaviors. Hope for the younger generation and for those of us who have bought into the hard-work-pays-off concept has been beaten down.

Besieged with financial, family, and work stresses, it is difficult to pinpoint the sources of what brings us joy and contentment. Where do we find pleasure and make each day happy and restful?

By contrast, spending time on a Caribbean island, one can see the simple life clearly: less stress, more joy and pleasure, more connection to one another, and less disruption and depression—especially when compared to the high expectations of Americans.

People on many islands no doubt have stress too, but their needs and wants appear to be more modest and realistic, and therefore more achievable. They do not have a carrot in front of their noses that they constantly chase but never catch. They appear to be satisfied with less, and instead focus on their free time, freedom, and family. Island families tend to remain close and connected.

The issue of achievability seems central to the attaining of satisfaction in our lives.

If we constantly need to reach higher and higher, in order to achieve more and more, will we ever find joy and satisfaction?

If our goals are modest and achievable, there is a far greater likelihood of success and satisfaction. That is not to say that the islanders do not also have goals and strive for a better life—or that they are lazy and satisfied with failure—but they seem to establish personal goals that are achievable instead of miles away. While we may define their lives as "simple" (by our standards, at least), is it really that or is it something else? Are others more realistic and, as a result, less subject to high levels of stress, anxiety, and depression?

Is it really "simple," or is it that their cultures are far more evolved, humane, and civilized?

Americans often define success as the acquisition of material wealth and financial security. I would argue that success is more related to the acquisition of personal feelings of esteem and self-satisfaction, based upon the use of our talents and capabilities, and not necessarily connected to money.

We can adjust our self-directed expectations here in America by not buying into the widely held ideas of success and achievement. Whether we're in a little village in the South of France, a small town in Jamaica, or a high-rise in downtown Chicago, we have the ability to create goals that yield satisfaction, and while these goals may be different in different places, they are unified in their achievability.

It is interesting to speculate why there is a huge push to leave home, especially when it is time to attend college. And while not everybody goes to college, there is a high value placed on setting out on your own and "making it happen" for yourself. There is high praise given to the person who leaves his native environment and becomes successful somewhere else. Young adults who remain at home when attending college are often looked at as perhaps not having the "goods" to make it on their own. There is the rationalization that experiencing some other locale is broadening and mind-expanding. While that may be true to a certain extent, there is also a clearly significant loss that results from that kind of thinking. A significant percentage of adults who move away from home to attend college frequently do not return to their native environment.

The idea of coming home after being away—whether for school or work—may feel like a "failure" to some. Somehow, the idea of returning to where your friends and family are located has become a low priority motivation. The far bigger motive is money: to go where you can achieve the most success, according to your particular definition of success. Not much value is given to the idea of returning to the family environment, which I think is a tremendous loss, and leads to family disruption, alienation, and serious loss of connection. Additionally, one of the motivations for going away is a new start. If you feel poorly about yourself, regardless of the reason, and feel that by staying home it will be hard to change people's perceptions of who you are, you will certainly be motivated to leave and start anew.

In contrast, the islanders mentioned earlier see the value of staying close to home, and while some of them may certainly leave home, they value coming home and being surrounded by family members—they are not looked upon as having failed. In fact, their homecoming is admired and valued enormously. The consistency and stability of the family structure is highly regarded, and anyone who respects and contributes to the family unity is loved for it. While in America coming home may be viewed as a negative factor, in other places it is seen as a significantly positive one.

Ultimately, it is a matter of psychological history. Where the integrity of the family structure is a positive feature and looked upon as a useful and valued factor, and where parents and authorities have insisted on the cohesion and integrity of family as some kind of priority, there will be a motivation to return to that structure and contribute to it.

But where the cohesion of the family structure is not idealized and seen as a valuable addition to one's life, there will be heightened levels of motivation to leave and diminished motivations to return. There is no doubt that this factor in American life has added to the slow disintegration of family priority and preeminence, and has even contributed to the diminished admiration for American culture, society, and civilization.

While islanders and others may lack many of the luxuries that we Americans can avail ourselves of, they always seem to have enough and are able to make do. I think we tend to look at that as diminished motivation and even laziness, when in fact we are failing to see the benefits that they obviously derive from staying close to their homes, families, and histories.

9

The Power of Human Connection, Part 1
Bonding

WE ALL UNDERSTAND THE GENERAL meaning of "connection." All of us seemingly long to have connections of a serious and intense nature. But what is it that facilitates and/or inhibits meaningful and deep connection amongst individuals? We often hear of people who report having deep and important connections to romantic partners, friends, even business partners or colleagues. We hear too of the very opposite of those who seem to be relatively unable, for a variety of reasons, to establish those types of close connections.

We seem to accept the idea that close and meaningful connections and relationships to others yields positive and reassuring feelings, and that an absence of those ties can result in a sense of futility, loneliness, and sadness. And it is clear that the disruption of close ties, for any number of reasons including death, acrimonious disruptions, or geographical distance, is a stressful and unsettling experience.

What is it that facilitates a sense of connection? While it is well-known that there are a number of different levels of connection, based upon intensity and depth, there seems to be common elements: the willingness to be open to others, and to trust in the integrity and honesty of one's connection to his partner or friend or colleague, are critical features and essential in determining and differentiating the levels to which any particular relationship can rise (or not rise).

When there are two parties desiring and capable of more openness and a willingness to expose their innermost feelings, the likelihood of more intense connection increases. And where there is hesitance of any kind in either person, there will be less chance of deep and long-lasting relationships. Individuals who have been massively traumatized or damaged in relationships in their past (especially where trust factors have been breached) will be less likely to be open and allow themselves to adopt vulnerable positions in order to connect with their partners.

The longing for a sense of completeness or "oneness" is common in the best of relationships. That does not imply vulnerability and a serious need for the "other" to provide basic and necessary structure for emotional equilibrium, but rather that the other is required for that heightened sense of togetherness and oneness. The nature of the connection needs to be balanced and equal in either direction, with both parties deriving enormous lifts in their self-awareness and sense of completeness. The relationship that has the potential for depth and real usable connection must be mutual and bidirectional. A connection between two individuals that is nurtured only by one of the parties cannot ever achieve that sense of fullness and completeness. At some point the provider will become frustrated and need to vacate that connection. It is only where the connection is fed equally from both parties can the sense of fulfillment and satisfaction be complete or long-lasting.

There are individuals who simply cannot go to those places that are essential for meaningful ties, namely, to allow themselves to take vulnerable and exposed positions in respect to others. Their self-system is so fragile that the goal is much more in the nature of self-protection than it is in creating deep relationships to others. Thus, these people will have little of substance to offer, and instead will seek connections where little is demanded or expected of them, except for perhaps certain surface or perfunctory functions that will suffice to keep the superficial relationship operational. These relatively "empty" people will not look for, recognize, or acknowledge relationships that are based upon deeper and demanding requisites. Instead, they can be easily satisfied by superficial needs.

Then there are the others who seek and are quite capable of connections that will matter and have the potential for life-changing and life-enhancing opportunities. They are eager, and not afraid to explore themselves; they are also deeply curious about others with whom they wish to have close ties. The feelings of openness and self-exploration and other explorations are exhilarating and intoxicating, and thus they are in search of those connections, although not in a "needy" manner. They will be available to those who also seek connections at moving levels of entanglement and involvement, and while not jumping in too readily, they will be amenable to exploring possibilities of significant interaction with others when presented with those options.

Being self-aware and able to empathize with others facilitates the potential for connections that change lives in meaningful ways and allows for important changes in life directions.

The search for a feeling of oneness is highly motivating for individuals who have the capacity to engage in high-level interactions with a partner. This is not motivated by a feeling of incompleteness, but rather by a search for higher levels of connection, and characterized by the sharing of time in mutual exploration, ideas and common interests, intimate and intense knowledge and "knowing" of each other, even the ability to accurately predict one another's reactions. People who experience that kind of closeness and unity will often feel and intuit their partner's next thoughts and ideas. I believe this to be the highest goal achieved within human interaction. The knowledge of the other is more—much more—than knowing a partner's favorite drink or meal or favorite color. It is knowing that person's mind, and sensibilities and sensitivities, as if they were your own—and caring about that partner and his or her well-being as if it were you going through the experience. When this kind of understanding is mutual and bidirectional, both parties come away from interacting feeling fuller, more energized, and self-satisfied in ways they may never have felt before.

If both parties are empathetic, they will make this most desirable type of connection that much more likely and enriching. What is most beautiful is that both individuals will have been able to expand their emotional and psychological horizons in a zone of great trust, honesty, and support, an essential milieu for growth and individual and independent elaboration of basic needs for one's self.

It is well-known, and for the most part believed (read Rainer Maria Rilke's *Letters to a Young Poet*) that the ultimate test of one lover's love for the other is the willingness and commitment beyond all others, to protect and facilitate the independent growth and development of the other lover. When the commitment is held sacred by both, and everything that can be done is done to ensure that outcome, both will be enormously enriched and expanded by that activity.

To have found that quality of interaction with your partner, and to feel the inevitable growth and emotional and psychological evolution, is to have found the secret to a peaceful and fruitful existence. This connection relies upon obtaining and seeking routine and predictable nurturing and refreshing of the relationship, but that process too is expansive for both parties. At times there may be fluctuating capacities to nourish from either side, but a well-oiled relationship will easily compensate for the inevitable variation in personal energies. But this too requires commitment without reservation from both parties.

10

The Power of Human Connection, Part 2
It's Personal

WITH THE INCREASING USE OF technology, every day we seem to interact less with our fellow human beings. While it is true that we may text, e-mail, or communicate on social media, direct and in-person contact has diminished in frequency and importance. The expediency of technology and the internet has made direct contact between people less common and as a result, less meaningful. To "get together" with your friends takes energy, planning, even sacrifice at times, but it takes almost no energy or time to send a text or make a comment on social media that communicates with your "friends." However, it is far less personal. The subtleties of human interaction are far less available and perceptible via social media, text, or e-mail. What is the eventual outcome of this phenomenon?

If direct contact with your friend or colleague—or even your spouse—is less valuable and takes up too much time, and a text or e-mail gets the job done in a split second, it is not hard to imagine that the value of human interaction and human communication will suffer enormously, if it hasn't been already. Most older folks amongst us still believe in direct communication as a way to contact friends and loved ones, partly because technology remains a puzzle that we have trouble solving. There was a time when a huge premium was placed on contact with your friends and close connections, but today that is seen as less valuable—or at least it appears that way. It bodes for the evolution of far less intimate relationships and connections amongst us. The lack of direct connection to others can easily precipitate a feeling of isolation, aloneness, and disillusionment with others. How did this gradual lack of communication happen? One could argue that communication has perhaps increased in some manner, because of the ease of connecting via smart phones and other devices, but I believe that those connections are of a depersonalized and even dehumanized sort.

We can blame the technology, but that may not be the whole story. It is more likely that the answer to that question lies more in the values that have evolved over time in our Western society. The rise of self-aggrandizement and self-importance, to the extent that we see it these days, has made interacting with others less relevant and gratifying. Others are far more important in their roles as admirers, validators, and sidekicks, but less important as confidantes, soul mates, and intimates. The rise of this feeling of "selfness" and the attention given to the enrichment of the self has taken over for mutual interaction, a process wherein both parties derive benefit from their connection. Unfortunately, the time taken to nourish and cultivate friendships and relationships is seen more as time away from one's own goals and aspirations, time you could instead be using to advance your own perspectives and narratives.

The disruption of powerful entities, whether the great empires of olden times, or the powerful and influential organizations of the present, has always been the evolution and idealization of selfness and self-serving behaviors, along with the devaluation of empathy, sensitivity, sharing, and concern for others.

This is not to dismiss the role of technology in this disintegration of important human values—in fact, as the technology advances and new ways of managing data and information emerge, the role of humans is dramatically diminished. Machines have taken over the ways we think, calculate, remember, and plan for the future. What has the role of ordinary humans become? Are we simply observers in the forward march of the machines? How will the evolution and further development of artificial intelligence affect our already limited roles? Will we simply be bystanders as the future unfolds in front of us?

It is impossible to predict how things will look and function twenty or thirty years from now, but the importance of the machine, not the human and his frailties and foibles, will likely be at the center of progress. Will there still be a place for human emotions, or will we become simple drones as in the novel *1984*? From the perspectives of those of us who have known other times, and lived in a world where empathy, understanding, sensitivity, and caring for others were valuable attributes, have those attributes and attitudes fallen onto the rubbish pile? Will there still be a place for those capacities between us, or will it all be something we simply do not do anymore?

How will children be raised, and how will relationships survive without those qualities? Will it all be based purely upon functionality and useful purpose? As children grow, at least in the experience of history, they require human qualities and sensitive interactions to develop souls and standards by which to deal with others. If connection is demeaned and portrayed as an unnecessary attitude, what will become of the capacity for working together, towards a common goal? What will happen to our concern for neighbors and colleagues? We are perhaps looking at a world of purpose, but without feeling and without a sense of unity amongst one another. How can this not ultimately lead to disintegration of any society, or any organization, regardless of size?

Hopefully, there will emerge a leader or a movement that rejects the self-centeredness of our present world. Without and until some charismatic individual or even an individual country comes along and espouses and embraces unity, we may well be doomed to proceed along our current pathway. If we are already on this path, we may be dangerously close to an inability to turn in a more positive direction.

It would be foolish to believe that machines have done all this to our world, but naïve to think that they have not contributed. Realistically it is us, humans, who have been seduced into believing that anything we can do to promote and push ourselves forward is acceptable behavior, no matter the cost to others or to the world around us.

Ask yourself, are we so far gone down that pathway to ultimate destruction and corruption of long-held values and standards by which to live that we cannot as individuals, make a turn for the better? I choose to believe that we can—if each of us considers the direction we are heading into and decides that there are more important issues than self-aggrandizement and power. We need to see the eventual outcome of the current direction we are headed in and redirect ourselves so we are recreating a world where empathy and love reigns supreme once again. We can cast the self-centeredness motive into the sea and regain and rediscover a world in which we can live peacefully and harmoniously with our fellow humans, and finally let go of our obsession with ego.

PART 2
AN EMOTIONAL CHARGE

11

Wanton Violence

IN ADDITION TO THE ABSOLUTELY riveting and stunning performance by Joaquin Phoenix, the film *The Joker* stood out to me because of a stark awareness of the role of violence in that film: wanton violence perpetrated upon people, regardless of their level of innocence. The reaction of many viewers was a mixture of being upset, repulsed, fascinated, curious, even afraid. The idea and crystal clear visualization of violence to that degree and in that manner was shocking, even to viewers who would rarely allow themselves to have the kind of angry and explosively violent feelings portrayed in the film. We can hypothesize that what makes people so upset or even repulsed by that degree of violence is the feelings it ignites in them: feelings that are generally deeply repressed and unavailable to them on a regular basis. As a society, we do not condone this kind of violent expression, or welcome the full-blown rage toward other human beings. In fact, we are very fearful of that kind of expression of violence, especially to the degree shown in the film, and we resist even fantasizing that kind of explosive anger.

Wanton violence refers to violence that occurs without just cause or obvious explanation; it is precipitous in nature, and often will cause serious physical and emotional trauma. Because it is usually unexpected, spontaneous, and without clear cause, the victim of such an assault is often subject to intense fear, a feeling of shock that the attack came out of nowhere. They are likely to be enormously traumatized by the event. The perpetrators of wanton violence are usually repeat offenders of this kind of behavior, and discharge their anger and explosiveness on convenient targets, often (but not always) totally unrelated to themselves. The targets of their violence may be completely random, they may have stimulated some memory or former experience, or they may have had certain attributes or characteristics.

What is going on internally in the mind of the perpetrator of wanton violence that lends to that kind of physical and emotional expression? Without any doubt whatsoever, the issue of the discharge of excess anger is at the center of this kind of behavior. These are individuals who, for whatever reason, have not been able to neutralize or manage angry emotions. There is a build-up of undischarged angry feelings that periodically will have to be discharged, and the target may be totally arbitrary. Managing anger is something that we learn early on in life. Parents who are able to effectively manage their own anger will be examples of such behavior to their own children. But parents who themselves are inefficient and ineffective in dealing with those feelings will, unfortunately, also act as an example for their children. And those children will internalize and identify (albeit unconsciously) with their parents' ways of handling emotions. There are certainly instances where that model does not hold up exactly: reasonable parents may in fact have a child who is different from them in critical ways, bringing his own style to the table. Rather than identifying with his parents' neutralized manner of dealing with pain or anger, he develops his own mode of discharge. This behavior sometimes results in the kind of violent behavior we are referring to. However, in general, individuals with explosive and angry character styles will have had some trauma somewhere along the way that facilitates their response. The cases where the differences between the child and his parents are markedly different are particularly interesting. It is not always clear or easily determined from whence stems that angry tendency, and that tendency toward explosive, violent behavior.

When the source of the outrage can be discovered, discussed, and explored in depth, individuals may have some opportunity to modify or modulate those behaviors. The problem is that these individuals often do not come to treatment until after catastrophic events have already occurred, making change that much more difficult. In many of the perpetrators of wanton violence, we often discover a history of their having been seriously abused and denigrated. As a result, the idea that an abuser has usually been abused themselves is valid. It is rare to see individuals with explosive, violent behaviors arise de novo, as if out of the dust. There is always a story, even if we do not always discover what it is.

As stated before, children learn to manage affects of all kinds, particularly negative ones such as guilt, shame, anger, sadness, hurt, and disappointment, from watching and internalizing the ways in which authority figures behave. Unfortunately, children are not able to carefully discriminate at an early age between what is beneficial and what is not regarding their futures. A child incorporates "in toto" what he sees—differentiation between what is useful and what is not comes much later in life. For some that difference never occurs: the intensity of the negativity is so great that even if he intellectually knows what is appropriate and what is not, there is no internalized self-control or ability to discharge negativity in balanced or neutralized ways.

For example, in the traditional sociopathic (psychopathic) personality structure an individual may well know what is right and what is wrong, but he is not guided or directed by that knowledge. Rather, he is driven by the undisciplined strength of his self-perceived desires. And it is important to note that the psychopath does not feel remorse or guilt of any kind, even when he knows he has done "wrong." Because he has no remorse or guilt, he will behave similarly the next time.

An individual with explosively violent behavior will not feel any kind of guilt or remorse about the effects he has on his victims. As stated above, he has a total lack of empathy and understanding of the pain and misery he is inflicting. In fact, he will often feel utterly justified in dealing out the punishment, and will find superficial and largely fallacious explanations to explain his violent reactions against others. There appears to be, in these more extreme examples of spontaneous violent behaviors, a dramatic lack of reality testing. There may even be delusional and illusional factors at play in choosing victims. This is not to say that every perpetrator of wanton violence is psychotic, but it always needs to be considered. Psychotic personalities, in the midst of an acute psychotic episode, can become violent for no perceptible reason—they are driven to that behavior by internally motivated emotions and misperceptions.

Historically, these particular personality characteristics are extremely difficult to treat or modify. They rarely come for help, and when they do, it is often driven by legal entities, and rarely by personal motivations and wishes for change and adaptation. The ability to perceive the effects of their behavior and function upon others is often absent, and they will be inordinately resistant to seeing their activities or violence as uncalled for. The psyche of these individuals is periodically simply overrun and overwhelmed with powerful angry affect that needs to be discharged, for fear of personally "exploding" should they do nothing. And that feeling of urgency and fear of psychological disruption and internal cohesion necessitates an immediate discharge, with the target being unimportant. Empathy, understanding, sensitivity to others are all totally eradicated in the face of that overwhelming need to discharge the painful accumulation of angry and explosive affect.

Much like the sociopath, the personal need for homeostasis and personal "gain" far outweighs the wish for reasonable and modulated behavior. This dynamic is also often seen in individuals with perverse needs, such as voyeurism, exhibitionism, child abuse, child molestation, fetishism, and others. Despite knowing their behavior is wrong, they cannot prevent themselves when the impulses become overwhelming, and they must then act, despite whatever the consequences might be.

12

The Price of Success

IN APRIL 2020, MY WIFE and I went for a walk around Chicago for some exercise and to remind ourselves that even during a pandemic, the world beyond our doors still existed and was likely to return to some kind of normalcy soon. At least that was our hope. We were impressed that there was only a fraction of the people we would normally see on the congested Chicago sidewalks, and that traffic in the streets was equally sparse. When we passed other pedestrians we all made a wide and sweeping pathway away from each other. We could not help but be mindful of distance and whether the people we came across were coughing or looked sick. Everyone out and about watched things one would ordinarily not notice, as if the "invisible enemy" lurked in the shadows, waiting to jump you if you were not cautious.

Unless you remain utterly isolated at home, your caution cannot completely protect you from potentially getting infected from others. So, even though we were walking, and to a certain extent enjoying being outside and not cooped up in the house twenty-four hours per day, there was a feeling of apprehension and awareness as we walked.

The feeling that day was one of danger everywhere, danger you could not see or detect—danger that could have even led to your death if the virus landed on you. Given that we have traversed these streets hundreds of times before, it was a strange and foreign feeling. There was a shared anxiety with most everyone else out there who, while not talking or sharing their worries with us, were most likely feeling the same way we did. The air had a paranoid feeling to it—you couldn't help but feel that everybody you passed had the potential to kill you, albeit unintentionally.

We turned off Michigan Avenue onto Oak Street, heading west toward Rush Street. This is an area of very high-end shops—Gucci, Prada, Dolce-Gabbana, Loro Piana—as well as a variety of jewelry stores and other fancy clothing shops and restaurants. It was a shocking and stunning scene to behold. Many of the shops, perhaps 60 to 70 percent, were boarded up or had significant protective coverings over their windows and doors. The street looked totally deserted, and reminded me of the ghost towns in those old movies about the Wild West. You could not help but feel both weird and uncomfortable by the site of these boarded up buildings that were ordinarily teeming with people and shoppers. Now, nothing. What was going on that we need these places to be boarded up and closed off, protected from intruders?

The answer to that question was—and is—obvious. These businesses were absolutely expecting that there would eventually be looters or people who would want to break into these shops and steal their merchandise for whatever reasons. The need for extreme protection is rampant on that street. Closed and locked doors are obviously not enough, at least based on what we saw on that block. I wondered if this is what we all need to expect now? Does this crisis my wife and I are in—that everybody is in—precipitate unruly and uncivilized behavior? Is it realistic to expect that as the crisis worsens and people become more desperate, they will feel entitled to break into someone's place of business, even their homes, and take what they need (or think they need) to survive? Is it really about survival, or simply about taking advantage of a crisis and an opportunity for wanton and uncivilized behavior? Will "boarding up" spread to other parts of Chicago, and will we see that kind of expectation spread? Those of us that live in this community are alert to dangers anyway and are ordinarily suspicious of unusual or strange looking individuals walking the street, but this degree of "paranoia" is uncomfortable and atypical.

What does it say about our society and community that there is this absolute expectation of violence and undisciplined behaviors? In checking the newspapers and the news in general, there was very little reporting of looting and breaking into stores in other countries, even though they are equally affected by the viral crisis. Countries like Italy, Spain, South Korea, and China have not reported wanton behavior like we experienced (and expected) here. What was the apparent difference? What makes Americans more likely to indulge in that kind of uncivilized behavior? What is it in our culture and society that facilitates and encourages that type of action?

If you look at leadership in America—at every walk of life, not just at the governmental level—we often see intensely self-directed and self-enhancing behaviors at every level, all of it condoned and even praised. The individual who seeks not to attain more power than he already has is seen as weak, wimpy, and non-ambitious—someone who is to be laughed at and ridiculed for his passive wishes. To be self-involved by taking care of yourself first and foremost (and to hell with the other guy) is de rigueur, and even expected. So how can we be surprised that when places of business are abandoned for obvious reasons—namely to protect us from the dreaded COVID-19 virus—the opportunity for aggressive individuals to take advantage of this opportunity presents itself. If I break that other guy's window and snatch a few watches for myself (that maybe I can then sell), why should I deny myself? After all, isn't that the credo of our country: to do whatever it takes to move ahead and put yourself in a position of power or having more material goods, no matter the cost to your fellow man? And, tough luck for the other guy who is an innocent victim of my avarice and greed, and my undisciplined and violent behavior.

The push towards having and getting and owning is so intense in the United States, and so much of what we call "success" hinges on the acquisition of material goods and tangible power, that the kind of rampant, violent behavior that is expected is almost a natural thing. But is it? Where is the civilized and philanthropic attitude of our fellow Americans? We see it in certain circles, but especially at a time when we are all under similar stresses like the coronavirus phenomenon, can't we share our resources and be available to our fellow man, instead of looking for ways to promote our personal circumstances? Can I take advantage of the opportunity to help myself at the same time I am hurting somebody else, and not caring about that in any way whatsoever? Where is the idea of sharing, caring, and concern for our fellow man? Aren't those the attitudes that make things better for everybody? Won't I feel better if I help that old man and his wife, my neighbors across the street, by bringing them groceries, and bringing in their paper every morning— will I feel better if I create a scam that cheats them out of their rent or grocery money?

The idea of sacrificing for your friend or neighbor, even if it costs you nothing except some time and energy, is not praised or honored. You may even be viewed as a sucker or fool if you do not take advantage of the chance to spring ahead in some way. Unfortunately, we do not praise that kind of behavior, although we certainly pay lip service to being a good person, one who is generous and philanthropic. But do we do that when we can? If I have a garden and grow tomatoes, you have a garden and grow carrots, and we choose to share our crops, we will both benefit by having a variety of vegetables on our table. But if I feel that you are either not being appreciative enough of my efforts or of my tomatoes, or that you are holding back on your carrots and taking advantage of my largesse, then I may retaliate by stopping the exchange, leaving us both deprived of that variety of veggies. It seems so obvious that the sharing of vegetables or resources of all kinds, including the sharing of energy, support, empathy, interest, and concern for one another, will allow us all to be far better off—we can all feel good about our contributions to the civilization of our society. But if those attitudes are seen as foolish or "sucker-like," we all suffer from not doing what seems so sensible and humane.

13

Why We Love Horror

THERE ARE SOME INDIVIDUALS WHO have a fascination
with horror of all kinds, whether it be in horror films—*Psycho, The Birds,
Nightmare on Elm Street, Ten Little Indians, The Fly*—or books. Often,
there is a preoccupation with human disaster or carnage in conjunction
with the horror films and books: Holocaust, school shootings, train
wrecks, or murder. Then there is the group of people at the opposite end
of the spectrum who are completely turned off by these scenarios, to the
extent that some may become overwhelmed with a feeling of revulsion
or nausea when witnessing such scenarios of tragedy. There is no doubt
that a wide range exists when it comes to how people view horror.

What is the seeming difference amongst those individuals? One
group is excited and even fascinated by scenes or indications of tragedy
and disaster—the other turns away and avoids them whenever possible.
There needs to be psychological and emotional explanations for this
apparent dramatic dichotomy. Are those who enjoy and seek catastrophe
truly sick? Are they so disturbed that their enjoyment comes from
experiencing tragic and horrifying scenarios? Or is there some clearer

and more precise explanation for their fascination with the macabre? Are those who consistently veer away from horror of all kinds perfectly balanced and live with total emotional equilibrium?

Let's explore plausible and possible explanations for these apparent differences—it's possible we may find that the emotional aspects of either group are not all that dissimilar.

Perhaps in the witnessing of horrifying scenarios, either real or fictitious, there is some release of tension, anger, voyeurism, pathological curiosity, and a resultant elevation of spirits. Perhaps it borders on the concept of "there but for the grace of God, go I." Clearly there must be some uplifting aspect to the activity, or it would not persist.

The fact of it being the "other" and "not me" is one aspect, but that does not address the discharge component of this action.

Because it is distant from the self, the experience affords the opportunity to feel one's rage, sadness, sense of tragedy, or sense of loss, but from a distance, thus making it far less poignant and painful. Yet there is vicarious pleasure in the discharge of negative and painful emotion.

Because the experience is not happening to you personally— therefore less threatening—the catharsis quality is intoxicating and at no personal cost, and without any personal embarrassment. Since these moments seem plentiful, they carry the promise of even more and more positive similar experiences. Because it's all just make-believe, there is even further protection from shame or self-disgust.

Keeping this in mind, those fascinated by the witnessing of horrific and tragic scenes may find some internal balance from having discharged negative and destructive feelings through a moment of passing identification with the perpetrators or victims of the horror. If it yields some modicum of heightened release, is it all bad? While on the surface it appears that people who enjoy horror and tragedy are ghoulish, hostile, even sick in their preoccupation with disaster and turmoil, if the result is heightened internal homeostasis, is that so bad? To be sure, an obsession with disaster and horror that interferes with normal life is clearly excessive and even psychologically pathological.

Is the other group that veers away from horror without allowing themselves any transient identification with the perpetrators or victims of that horror—preserving internal balance or running away from imbalance and from feelings that they judge as abhorrent, repulsive, or negative? Is their distance from horror really a statement of fear and repression, rather than one of decency? Here too there is a significant issue of degree. Total absence from any momentary identification with these moments suggests anxiety, fear, and suppression of feeling. This group is too afraid and unwilling to even temporarily allow themselves to go "there."

In both groups, feelings that are stirred up are not all that different— what is different is the way in which they are managed. One group dives in, seemingly enjoying the water, while the other sticks to walking along the beach out of fear of being overwhelmed, even momentarily.

14

The Truth About Mourning

WHILE WE USUALLY CONSIDER THE process of mourning something directly related to the loss of a loved one, mourning occurs in a variety of situations, and is no less painful and disruptive. The acute loss of a loved one—partner, spouse, grandparent, close friend, or even a beloved pet—is the mourning we usually identify with. But there are losses of many kinds that can precipitate a state of mourning. The loss of a business, the end of a successful career, leaving college, the hope of an opportunity that never materializes, and the idealized hopes and aspirations for ourselves or for our children that never come to fruition are all events that can lead to mourning. While these are not the usual precipitants to mourning, they do in fact cause intense feelings of loss, sadness, and frustration, and can develop into a protracted state of distress.

The issue of unrequited aspirations for ourselves, our children, or close associates, and the connection of those aspirations to mourning, is something we do not always pay attention to. We don't always pay attention to the degree of suffering often associated with these types of disappointments. Raising children with expectations and aspirations is a normal, even required aspect of parenting. It is critical for parents to have some kind of idealized image for their children, but that image should be based upon knowing the child, including their aptitudes and proclivities, so that the child has something attainable to strive for Children are driven by attainable goals, goals that are specific to them and their skill sets and interests. The likelihood of success is intimately connected to the proximity between the skills of an individual and the goals they have set for themselves (or ones that have been set for them by others).

We often can see the lack of appreciation for particular interests or aptitudes of children—parents will set goals that are not in sync with the individual directions of their children. Instead, the goals for their child may be set to encompass the unsatisfied and unfulfilled wishes of the parent and have little or nothing to do with the child. Needless to say, this establishes a situation guaranteed to fail and disappoint, in both the child and parent(s). The disappointed reaction in either can feel like the death (of a fantasy), and thus a feeling of mourning can be easily experienced.

All too often parents will feel disappointed in their child, irrespective of the child's success in a particular area, but unless there is a coalescence of the child's activity and the parents' wishes for that child, there can still be a sense of loss and sadness over the unrequited wish for the child. Not only does that situation cause parents to feel sad and mourn, it can also precipitate a feeling of loss and disappointment in the child: the child will feel their parent's disappointment and feel like they have failed them. As you can see, mourning can occur at both ends of that connection. In parents, the feeling is the result of their unfulfilled wishes that they were hoping might be gratified vicariously through the success of their child. Instead they are left feeling loss and even anger. In the child, the fantasy of satisfying their parents gets dashed, as that child correctly perceives that their parent is upset about their lack of success or achievement.

Classical mourning reactions, except in certain cases, do not have an associated guilt aspect. They are characterized by loss, sadness, and eventually by anger at the loss (really anger at having lost the object of potential future gratification). Those cases where guilt plays some part is where there remains some ambivalence or conflict in connection to the lost object or activity. It is well known that guilt in those situations will generally prolong the mourning process, and where the guilt is not a part, the reaction of loss and mourning goes more quickly and without conflict. Completion of the mourning process is more difficult when the feeling of guilt is stronger. Since there is no real way to resolve the remaining conflict (with the lost object) there can be a residual feeling of incompleteness.

In the situation discussed above in which lost hopes and dreams for a parent and their child exist—and where at least one of the parties in the interaction feels guilt—resolution is also much more difficult and time-consuming. With a more personal loss of one's hopes and dreams, it is possible to conduct some helpful self-analysis and self-reflection, and thereby come to some homeostasis internally. However, when there are two (or more) parties involved in the loss and disappointment, open discussion is clearly required to come to some kind of resolution. In situations such as these, where there is no reasonable possibility of discourse and eventual re-establishment of equilibrium, there can remain a long-standing feeling of bitterness and even anger at one another. Not only is there a persistent feeling of disappointment in the failed hopes and dreams of both parent and child, there is also the loss of some essential tie in the relationship itself (which can lead to a feeling of mourning).

Similarly, when one feels they have not lived up to certain aspirations and expectations they held for themselves, there is certainly a significant aspect of disappointment and at times, even a strong self-castigating quality. Because we are often encouraged to stretch or extend ourselves beyond what is realistic, we can easily make the goal of achievement and success close to impossible. While it is sometimes true that one can achieve far more than ever expected, that is the exception. It is more common to experience undershooting one's goals, especially when those goals are unrealistic. Just as it is important to set attainable goals for our children, so too is it for ourselves. The failure of an expectation, especially when the level of success is far below what was hoped for or expected, can lead to a mourning process, primarily grieving the loss of self-esteem, loss of judgment in setting too-high goals, and anger at having missed the target, no matter how unrealistic.

The resolution of mourning reactions requires at least two important steps:

1. There needs to be an acceptance of the loss of the fantasy or the loss of the departed object. Everyone involved must come to accept that the wishes and goals may have been unrealistic and could not have been accomplished, and they must come to terms with the disappointment. Both will suffer, and that is normal.

2. There needs to be an acceptance that there can no longer be any possible gratification from the attachment to that object, activity, or fantasy. There can still be positive and pleasant memories that persist, having occurred with the lost object, but nothing new or satisfying will be coming.

The second step is a hard one to take, but once you do, mourning will quickly come to a close. Using Freud's analogy of soldiers left to protect hidden fortresses (i.e., unresolved past conflicts), once the idea has penetrated that there is no possible gratification or satisfaction that can occur from the lost object, the soldiers (energy and connection to the lost object) will be pulled away and able to "join the front lines" in the day-to-day struggles of life, but with heightened energy, enthusiasm, and freedom.

A mourning reaction is most commonly seen with the death of a loved one. Of tremendous difficulty is that aspect of grieving and mourning that necessitates the acknowledgment of anger over the loss. All too often people confuse this anger as if it is directed at the departed person, and therefore feel uneasy or even guilty at having angry thoughts at all: "How can I blame them for dying and leaving? They didn't do it purposely or to make me feel bad." The fact is, as stated above, that anger is really directed at lost future gratification and satisfaction.

In fact, this raises a very important issue: that the loss of future (that is an absolute loss of any future interaction—positive or negative—with the departed person or object) is part of the anger that surviving individuals struggle with. But the recognition that there is nothing more to be gained by maintaining an active connection to the departed person or object, through ongoing hopes and wishes, is what leads directly to the dissolution of the mourning reaction, and unleashes the ability to move forward.

The resolution of a mourning reaction is very often accompanied by a tremendous upsurge of energy and good feeling. While the sadness over the loss will not totally disappear overnight or perhaps ever, there is a shift in focus to the life ahead and the possibilities of future satisfaction and joy, and away from a preoccupation with the losses suffered.

15

Nirvana on Earth

BEFORE A TRIP TO SOUTHEAST Asia, my wife and I had not really been exposed to the Buddhist religion (perhaps more properly thought of as the Buddhist philosophy) in a significant way—what we experienced was a very impressive phenomenon unfolding before our eyes.

Most people are aware of the vicissitudes and variants found within the Judeo-Christian religions, but to us, aspects of Buddhism appeared amazing, extremely attractive, and very different from what we knew— all in a profound way. The basic premises of the majority of religions are generally the same: be good to one another, be generous with what you possess, take care of your brothers and sisters and try to avoid being excessively self-occupied and selfish, and abide by rules of decorum and civility. Based upon what we witnessed, Buddhism was no exception, but there is so much more at the center of this philosophy. There is a drive towards central calmness and peacefulness, which is palpable, obvious, and powerful. The willingness to provide for others, even at the cost of one's own discomfort or deprivation, appears to be a notable motivation and source of emotional reward.

In observing the monks, what jumps out is their softness, gentleness, and willingness to give to their fellow man—even if they own nothing, possess nothing, and have only their prayers to offer. Their actions are done with complete willingness, and you can feel the authenticity of their "gifts"—totally genuine and touching. It begs the obvious question: Why is this behavior seemingly restricted to these Buddhist individuals and in general to the practitioners of Buddhism? There is absolutely no room for narcissism and for self-centeredness in Buddhism. You cannot find evidence of that blight on humanity in any practitioners of that religion. They do not know it, honor it, praise it, seek it, or value it. Thus, their pleasure comes not from self-aggrandizement, but from acts of generosity and giving to others, and from the discovery of a central place of peace within themselves. In fact, it appears that self-centeredness would be cause for abandoning Buddhist principles, and joining the Western world and its preoccupation and respect for self-enhancing and self-promoting behaviors. It is not that they seek deprivation, but deprivation is a way of self-discipline and learning what is truly important in life, namely the attainment of inner peace and tranquility. We learn from Buddhism that serving is a useful and valuable goal for yourself and humanity. The usual actions of Westerners and of practitioners of Judeo-Christian religions are far from those Buddhist goals. The need for the acquisition of *possessions*, *power*, and *position* appears to vastly outweigh the seeking of inner peace and calmness and stands as a serious obstacle to the obtaining of what Buddhists seek and find.

Could we not all adopt a little of those goals for ourselves, and find a way to make peace and inner calm a major standard to strive towards? Can we give up the insane quest for superiority and power that seems to drive us and intoxicate us? The intoxication is toxic and self-destructive, and eats away at our humanity, generosity, and willingness to embrace our fellow man and discover what true peace, community, and love is about. And by our focus on self and self-enhancement in a wide range of modalities, we avoid and miss out on the benefits of inner calm and peace that come from a gentle and loving worldview.

To obtain the Buddhist sense of nirvana seems possible, but the active pursuit of personal possessions, power, and position will by necessity preclude and obstruct your entry into that tranquil and beautiful inner space.

It is not to say that everything about our Western world and lifestyle lacks value, but we seem at times to lack the capacity for balance. There is nothing inherently wrong with wanting to be successful (through utilization of our God-given talents and capabilities), but too often that drive to succeed excludes any recognition and valuing of the calmer side of life. Unfortunately, we Westerners too often associate seeking calmness and looking for a peaceful place within ourselves as missing out on opportunities for success, and instead as laziness or lack of motivation.

This is a serious mistake. Both can be achieved, but it is not a simple task. Seeking balance in life, which I believe is at the center of Buddhist thinking, is a desirable life plan for all of us. At the same time as you are enjoying a peaceful inner existence and finding a calm place in your heart and soul you can also be exploring and actualizing your parallel drive to be successful, depending on what your own definition of success is. The two do not need to be mutually exclusive. As long as we see the drive for inner calm and peace as replacing the actualization of our drive for achievement, the pursuit of that calm place inside will not happen.

It is relevant to note, that while the Buddhists appear to be seeking and discovering that internal place of peace, they are still productive and working very hard, albeit with vastly different goals than we Westerners have. Their work is in the service of others, maintaining their communities and seeing that food for the belly and the mind is at the forefront of work activity. They work no less hard than we do, but their goals of work and productivity are vastly disparate from ours. It is extremely important to have had a role model that exhibited that capacity for balance at some time during our lives. If you were raised in a household and in an environment where productivity was the single most important goal, then to seek calm and peace will not fly. But if you were raised in a household that exemplified a balanced approach, then you too were able to pursue those goals and given license to identify with those goals. Sadly, in our Western world—unlike what we witness in the Eastern world where Buddhism rates so highly—we seem to eschew and avoid the movement towards that dual set of goals for ourselves. When we have leaders or models that see productivity and economy as the principle values to work towards, that other side of life—the one that grants us inner tranquility and self-satisfaction—will not be pursued as easily as it might. It is a sad statement about our modern-day Western world that we miss out on what could be that "nirvana on earth" the followers and practitioners of Buddhism so actively seek.

16

Mid-life Crises

T HE CONCEPT OF MID-LIFE crisis is one that is easily bandied about, but often poorly understood. Generally speaking, it pertains to individuals of a particular age—usually around fifty—who are having trouble feeling good about where they currently are in their lives. This is not to say that crises of this type do not happen at other ages as well, but we seem to focus on that age—an age at which we begin to see that life does not last forever and time is running out. But running out for what reasons?

The typical question we ask ourselves when suffering through this "crisis" is: "Is this all there is? I have worked all these years, hoping and wishing for a certain kind of life, but life has not provided me what I hoped for, I planned on, or expected." As a result, and based on our expectations, we feel disappointment, disillusionment, and even depression (especially if the situation is serious enough).

The central issue of this phenomenon seems to be achievement (or lack thereof) of deeply held, long-ago established wishes and expectations we had for ourselves. The degree to which we have achieved these unconsciously held goals and dreams determine the extent of our disappointment and disillusionment. The issue of success is often at the epicenter of this crisis, but the exploration of people suffering with this condition reveals that there are a multitude of issues that can give rise to our feelings of underachievement. In some ways, our wishes and expectations are more similar than not: We all want to be loved, respected, admired, successful (including financially and in relationships), recognized, and valued. Most importantly, we want to feel good about ourselves.

In many instances, even when there is external admiration and respect directed at us, unless we feel that achievement internally (especially in areas that are most important to us), that external recognition will not impact our self-esteem and self-feeling. Thus, the most critical issue is the extent to which we feel satisfied with our performance and achievements in a variety of areas. Success in one area (i.e., financial) will not make up for a sense of failure or lack of achievement in other areas (i.e., relationships). There needs to be a feeling of balance and self-acknowledgment in all the areas that we deem relevant for ourselves as unique individuals. And these areas of relevance may vary widely amongst us.

Generally, when we think of mid-life crises, we often direct that diagnosis at men. However, women are also subject to this condition. The goals and aspirations of women are as powerful and meaningful to them as goals and aspirations are to men. Women may define success and achievement in different ways than men do, but they are nonetheless subject to similar disappointment and depression should their goals and achievements fall short. The sense of "Is this all there is?" is relevant for both sexes. For many of us, men and women alike, the idea of long-held aspirations for ourselves not actually working out is almost by definition a disappointment. But the question arises: how do the goals and expectations get established by men or women?

We know that a critical role parents play in raising their children is to help them establish realistic and attainable goals and aspirations. These goals, which are set up very early in a child's life, will drive and push him or her throughout their life, so the necessity for understanding and having sensitivity to the particular aptitudes and skill sets of that child are essential. To establish goals that are disassociated and non-specific to a particular child is to assure future frustration and disappointment. However, helping a young child develop aspirations and expectations for himself or herself that are in keeping and alignment with his proclivities and interests can help lead to a more fulfilling and well-rounded lifestyle.

If you have set up unrealistic and unattainable goals for yourself, you are courting a potential disastrous self-assessment later in life. This clearly sets the stage for future disappointment and even depression if the shortfall is great enough. While it is true that self-assessment and self-evaluation go on throughout someone's life, at certain stages we become more focused on it. For example, we all can relate to the milestone birthdays (i.e., thirty, forty, fifty) as a time of self-assessment. Why mid-life crises typically occur around fifty years of age may be related to other issues: As stated earlier, it is a time when we begin to realize that life is finite, and that time is a major factor going forward. If we want to really achieve the goals we have set for ourselves, the time to do that is not endless. The recognition that life is not forever is a major moment in one's life—not that we don't know that we will all one day die and no longer be around, but the reality of that fact does not normally impress us until later in life. It is hypothesized that the recognition of that loss of immortality is the major factor precipitating a mid-life crisis, and unconsciously forces us to assess our levels of achievement. We ask ourselves, "If time is not infinite, where am I on that spectrum of success and the goals I have set for myself to achieve in my lifetime?"

It is human nature to not exactly hit the goals we have set for ourselves. There may be the occasional individual who does, in fact, reach the peak of his or her aspirations, but that person is the exception. The majority of us will have fallen short in certain areas, and that precipitates that sense of disappointment and creates feelings of "I have worked so hard to be successful in the ways I have outlined for myself, but have fallen short." The question we end up asking ourselves is: "Is this all there is, and is this paltry sense of accomplishment the only reward I will receive for all my hard work?"

Additionally, there is the growing awareness that because time is fleeting, we are not who we were twenty-five to thirty years ago— teeming with boundless energy, a sense of infinite options to choose from, a booming level of self-esteem—and a realization that my drive towards successful goals achievement may not be as intense as it once was. How will I ever achieve the goals I set out for myself earlier in life? That awareness precipitates a sense of anxiety and fear, and self-questioning: "Of what real worth have I been to myself and to others?"

It is therefore easy to see that the growing awareness and realization of the perceived closing down of options, and the diminished energy to pursue those dreams, can give rise to a feeling of loss, sadness, and even despair, leading to a mid-life crisis.

Unfortunately, the crisis might not stop at mid-life. We could coin a term, but not a new concept—old-age crisis. This would be the feelings and self-assessments we make at an older age, but also at the proverbial "death-bed" scenario: "How have I fared over the course of my lifetime?

Have I achieved what I thought I would? Have I left an admirable legacy for myself and my family, colleagues, and associates? How do I feel about myself after a careful self-appraisal? Am I accepting of the accomplishments I did achieve, without criticism and without remorse for the ones I have not achieved? Or am I distraught of all that I have not done and promised myself I would try to do in my lifetime? Can I give myself credit for the efforts and achievements I did manage over time, or am I focused primarily upon the shortfall?"

This reaction in older age or even at death's door is also fashioned early on in life. If the ego ideals (life's goals) that were either set for you by outside authorities (like your parents) or in conjunction with your own self-perception, with adequate room made for the inevitable failures of achieving everything you were shooting for, then you will not feel full of remorse, embarrassment, and self-denigration, either at the time of "mid-life crisis" or "old-age crisis." But if the ego ideals were set up with little or no room for failure, then the remorse and humiliation will be far more intense and painful.

If the focus of activity is always upon final outcomes and not upon the efforts made in achieving internally established goals, then this becomes a formula for disappointment and even despair later on. The ability to determine and manage the inevitable gap between what we were shooting for and what we actually achieved and accomplished will, in the final analysis, determine the comfort level at any stage of self-appraisal and self-assessment. That ability will have been established early on but could change over time to a certain degree—if we are aware and self-reflective enough to realize that we are chasing unattainable goals. As a result, we have the ability to adjust our aims, even at a later stage of life, to more achievable and attainable aspirations. That ability to make changes later in life to more reasonable aims and aspirations (with the goal of feeling more successful and more self-satisfied) is not an easy task, but we need to become aware of the futility of pursuing unreasonable goals at any stage of the game. And in that recognition of futile efforts being made we can be driven to self-examine and make the essential changes to more sensible and attainable ambitions.

17

The Delusion of Fantasy

AT A PERFORMANCE OF *MADAMA Butterfly* at the Lyric Opera in Chicago, a particular dynamic familiar to many of us jumped out and made itself crystal clear. While it was relatively easy to identify the particular psychological constellation, to understand the underlying emotional and dramatic pathology of this dynamic is not so obvious nor easy to negotiate.

The dynamic that jumped out was the willingness for one partner to develop and embrace a fantasy associated with their partner, and to nourish, believe in, and defend the perfection of that other. Regardless of the clarity and truth of a contradictory set of factoids and information, this perception holds.

That individual—the "holder" and "embracer" of the idealized fantasy—will defend to preserve and even enhance the fantasy. In the case of *Madama Butterfly*, the fantasy was defended to death. It seems so obvious for outsiders viewing this behavior to see its folly, but to those experiencing it, it is not as clear.

So the question arises, how does this level of fantasy happen? The creation of such a fantasy can often lead to enormous sacrifice and deprivation on the part of the creator. If the idealized partner should fail in any perceptible manner, the creator will always see that as their shortcoming, thereby preserving the perfection of the idealized object. The length that the creator will go to in order to preserve the fantasy is almost infinite. In certain cases, the deprivation, pain, disappointment, and disillusion are so profound that even a truly delusional thought process cannot save and resurrect the delusional fantasy. In those cases where there is a sudden and precipitous clairvoyance, it will be accompanied by monumental sadness, loss, emotional devastation, depression, and anger.

What is the need of the "creator" to rationalize that fantasy? It must be related to the view the creator has of himself. A fully esteemed individual will not need to create idealized others to buttress and enhance their own feelings of themselves. They will not be influenced by association with others who are powerful or masterful. Instead, they are able to realistically see themselves as they are, willing to tackle their own shortcomings and weaknesses. They are able to capitalize on their idiosyncratic capabilities and proclivities and do not need to create power and perfection in others associated with them (even in tangential ways) in order to feel better about themselves. They are able to adjust and adapt their behaviors based upon reality and find better and more efficient and effective patterns that ultimately enhance self-esteem, without interference or reliance upon their immediate external environment.

Is this a learned behavior, genetic inbreeding, or simply an adaptation to what must have been a painful past? Was adopting an idealized view of those around us a way of survival preserving emotional integrity, even if it was at enormous personal cost?

It is interesting to speculate why, despite clear evidence that the idealized object is flawed and imperfect, the creator of the fantasy cannot give it up. There is perhaps a fear that if you abandon the fantasy of connection with the object of perfection, you will, in some critical manner, disintegrate yourself and never feel whole again. That fear may be irrational, something that at times is utterly inexplicable and overtakes the psyche, seemingly paralyzing its ability to see the truth, relegating the sufferer to be totally consumed and immobile.

The ever-present fear of a disintegration of the cohesive self will promote infinite levels of subservience and subjugation of the individual and will disallow any possibility of dealing with the inevitable truth of the situation. The longer the self-deception goes on, the greater the adherence to the fantasy and the less likely it will ever be examined in an honest and clarifying manner. It becomes a psychological trap without an escape. Even the descent into psychosis, a phenomenally painful solution, does not allow the fantasy holder to escape.

The whole concept of delusional thinking has application in a variety of situations. But one such situation in which it plays a major part is where there is an environment of abuse, either emotional or physical. The delusional aspect of this phenomenon is the activity of the abused party in relation to their abuser. There is very often a totally blind eye turned towards the abuse, and in fact the activities of the abuser are often even rationalized and found (by the abused) to be justified for the alleged "wrongdoing" or offensive actions of the abused. In other words, the abused victim will make all kinds of excuses as to why they were abused and even perhaps deserved the abusive treatment from their partner.

What are the underlying psychological and emotional motives for allowing that kind of mistreatment to go on? Why doesn't the abused person not see what is obvious to everybody else? How does the abuser (who usually has a long history of that kind of behavior) find his victims? What are the signs and alerts that allow the abuser to pick someone who will easily tolerate and suffer his abuse? It is also true that an abused individual probably has a long history of similar experiences in their own past, and gravitates towards individuals who are only too willing to impose their will on a vulnerable victim.

And curiously, the abused will rarely see themselves as a victim, Instead, they often see the abuser as a victim of their history and past, and will go to the nth degree to understand, nurture, forgive, and cater endlessly to their abuser's wishes. Very frequently the abused one will see themselves in the role of a savior for one who has suffered terribly in their past. The result is that the abused individual indirectly becomes a hero in their own mind. And the abuser will facilitate and nourish that idea in their victim.

The psychology of the abused victim is often based upon certain deeply-held believed delusions. The abused person creates a fantasy about their partner that they want to believe is true—they stick to this idealized fantasy, even in the face of contrary and convincing evidence. The abused person does not want to admit to themselves the error of their choice and will defend their choice even when it involves further suffering and denigration. The need to be right about their choice, and to continue to see their abuser as idealized and perfect in many ways, is how the delusional thinking occurs.

It is not that an abused person consciously or unconsciously seeks abuse—instead, they do not properly identify and react appropriately to it when it does occur.

The need to preserve their idealized fantasy is so great that reality is grossly distorted in order to save the perceived perfection of their partner and maintain some internal homeostatic equilibrium. The fear is that if someone recognizes the abuse for what it really is, and the abuser for who they really are, their world will come crashing down. This fear of emotional disintegration is what motivates the need to keep the fantasy alive, despite obvious evidence to the contrary. This fear of the massive internal disruption is mostly overstated, but the abused person cannot allow themselves to see that and will do almost anything to maintain the connection with the abuser—and with the fantasy that they have created about that person.

This is why, when an abused person sees that their abuser is pulling away, regardless of the reason, they will do anything to preserve the relationship—no matter the cost to themselves or the extent to which they will have to subjugate themselves going forward. They are willing to do almost anything to keep things going. The level of vulnerability and willingness to sacrifice oneself and take on any personal cost to maintain that connection is the seat of the delusional thought. To have the abuse pointed out by a concerned or caring observer will be of no real use. In fact, it will be seen as a lack of understanding by that observer.

As in *Madama Butterfly*, it is better to die by one's own hand than see the truth about the delusional thought process. While the abused person may not commit suicide, there will be a death-like, life-abandoning commitment to the relationship. And if, for whatever reason, the abuser abandons his victim at some point, perhaps because they have found a new victim and a new challenge, the abused person will always feel that they have chased the abuser away because of their behavior, lack of support, or lack of understanding. To come to the real reason of why the abuser left will be torturously difficult to accept, and incredibly painful to deal with.

18

Dealing with Catastrophe

"CATASTROPHE" COMES FROM THE GREEK word *katastrephein*, meaning "an overturning." *The Merriman-Webster* dictionary defines catastrophe as "an event causing great and sudden damage or suffering."

As we age, the likelihood of catastrophe and catastrophic events becomes increasingly likely. While it is not totally a function of age, it is simply that the longer we are around, the greater the likelihood of some damaging event occurring. The nature of catastrophic events can vary widely, and depending on the nature, severity, duration, and outcome of these events, will determine the impact and significance to the individual suffering such an experience.

The more typical catastrophic events could be classified as either externally motivated or internally motivated. That is, the event can come from without, such as the sudden loss of a loved one, the loss of one's business, the loss of substantial sums of money and security, and the precipitous and inexplicable ending of a long-standing friendship or relationship, to name a few. Internal catastrophic events can be characterized as coming from within, and while generally less common, may sometimes be even more devastating. Examples of such catastrophes would be acute losses in self-esteem that can come from a multitude of sources: being exposed as a thief, discovering hidden family secrets of a negative and formerly unknown nature, loss of significant relationships based upon one's own misbehaviors, and public humiliation for a variety of misdeeds.

It is obvious that external catastrophic events can also have internal ramifications. In fact, it is very likely that whether the catastrophe comes purely from without or purely from within, they will often be overlap.

Catastrophic events are characterized by their sudden and unexpected occurrence, lack of preparedness in the sufferer, intensity of emotion and pain evoked in the victims, traumatic levels of emotional overload, and feelings of shock and surprise by those involved. In situations where the catastrophe is, for example, a devastating diagnosis such as pancreatic cancer, the individual receiving the diagnosis as well as those around them will all be dramatically impacted by the news. As stated above, the nature of the catastrophe, duration, severity, and outcome will ultimately define the impact upon those involved. The more intense the negativity of the event and the longer it lasts, the greater the damage and suffering inflicted upon the participants.

The nature of an individual's response to catastrophe and cataclysmic events is determined by a number of factors. Probably the most important is the nature of the individual's personality and any former experiences they have had with similar events, even if the events are different in nature. In some ways earlier similar experiences both insulate one against devastating reactions and make reactions more intense. For example, when individuals have already experienced traumatic and unexpected events—and have managed those events effectively—they will most likely be much more resilient and responsive to the new assault. If those former traumatic events have been either repressed or denied—and essentially not dealt with—that individual is likely to have a more disruptive and emotionally overwhelming reaction to the next catastrophic moment.

How we react to and handle catastrophic events may be more easily managed as we age, because we likely have confronted situations over the course of our lives that have tested our resilience, psychological infrastructure, and ability to see "the light at the end of the tunnel." We have been here before, and know how this will eventually turn out, so we prepare ourselves for that eventuality. Needless to say, we can make serious misjudgments and misconceptions, based often upon our wishes for a more positive outcome, ending up hopelessly lost when the outcome is different from what we were expecting. But as with most things in life, we learn from our experiences and are generally less surprised and fooled even by cataclysmic moments.

The ability to effectively react to sudden and traumatic moments is essentially a function of what we learned in childhood (and beyond) combined with experience. As mentioned above, the more experience we have in dealing with catastrophe, especially when it comes to learning to deal with it effectively, the better prepared we will be for the next sudden and devastating event. But it is during childhood that we truly build the psychological infrastructure that will prepare us to more effectively deal with disruptive and devastating moments, be they our personal catastrophes or in those around us.

It has been said that the single most important function of parenting is helping and teaching our children to deal with affect, especially intense affects, both positive and negative. Inability to deal in a masterful way with affects, both negative and positive, renders a child vulnerable to overwhelming and devastating reactions in the future. When I talk of the important affects and emotions that we must teach our children to manage well, I refer to intense feelings: joy, passion, celebration, disappointment, loss, abandonment, serious loss of self-esteem, anger, guilt, shame, sadness, and depression. The degree to which children have been taught to deal effectively with intense emotions that none of us can ever escape completely, the better prepared they will be to deal with these feelings in constructive ways. There is always the possibility that children will experience such intensity of pain and suffering later on that even with excellent counsel by parents they can be overwhelmed. However, they will recover faster and more effectively over the long run with strong and early guidance. How can we achieve this?

We would all swear that we are bound and determined to show our children the right road to happiness and fulfillment: good self-esteem and balanced, predictable behaviors, including their being able to deal with their feelings in constructive ways. But how is that accomplished?

Children learn from watching their parents (and other adults), and not from what they hear from them. We all have excellent intentions, and want nothing but the best for our children, but they learn by observing how we manage affects. The overly angry father should not be surprised when his son or daughter also has anger problems, or the sociopath (with limited impulse control) should not be surprised when his child is arrested for stealing at the local pharmacy or is apprehended for selling marijuana. The chronically depressed mother should not be surprised when her daughter also begins to complain of sadness and uncontrollable suicidal urges. Or the high school dropout, who had trouble concentrating and motivating himself in a school setting, should not be surprised when his child declares that college is useless, enlisting in the army instead. We lead by example, and not by what we say to our children. The shame-prone parent will introduce his children to dealing poorly with disappointment and potentially shameful experiences of all kinds.

And while they can be modified with intense work and psychological understanding, the ways of dealing with feelings and emotions that we learn early in life remain in place as the basic infrastructure of our personality going forward. It is what we learn early on that ultimately determines how we react when catastrophe befalls us later in life. However, we are fortunate that through the acquisition of wisdom and vigilant examination and reflection, and by considering carefully what has (and hasn't) worked for us when dealing with emotional charge, we may still be able to slowly alter our basic responsiveness to emotions and emotional overload of all kinds, finding new ways to deal more effectively with feelings and affects.

It is well-known that children can sometimes be extremely resilient in managing catastrophic situations: the unexpected loss of a parent, serious physical illness in themselves or a loved one, dramatic changes in circumstance (such as parental divorce, or moving to another city). While not all of these situations are hugely negative in nature, they still require significant adaptation. It is also well-known that internal emotional strength comes through the management of adversity of all kinds. The more adverse a situation, the more possible it is for relevant and dramatic adaptation as well as the development of reliable emotional infrastructure.

Children seem to be more resilient than adults in many circumstances, not only because of a lack of understanding of the world around them. They may have a deeper, even naïve, belief in the goodness of mankind and the fruitfulness of the world around them. They have not yet become jaded and can therefore more easily see the possible positive outcomes than adults who have lived lives in which disappointment and failure are more well-known, and even expected. Having said that, there are adults we could characterize as "pure-hearted" because they see the world in a more idealized manner, and like children, may react more favorably to catastrophe because of their more positive outlook.

The premise stated earlier in this chapter—that children learn from their parents about the handling of crises and intense affects of all kinds—is not being dismissed. Even without appropriate role modeling, young children may still be able to handle acute crisis situations effectively because of their positive outlook on life. This concept does not disregard the fact that Post-Traumatic Stress Disorder (PTSD), an intense psychological reaction to acute trauma, can still be found in a wide range of individuals with varying basic personality structures. The development of PTSD is not necessarily restricted to the "weaker" personalities.

In fact, it is curious that in acute crisis situations, where a number of individuals are exposed to the same traumatic event, some of them might develop PTSD while others do not, and the difference in emotional responses is often inexplicable, given that they have all been exposed to the same toxic stimulus. The answer may clearly be related to earlier experiences with traumatic circumstance in the person's life.

The more capable one is in managing crises early in life, the more adequately prepared that person will be to manage them later on. Similarly, where a child or young adult is massively overwhelmed by catastrophe, and has not made adequate adaptive changes to the crisis, he will be that much more vulnerable to future moments of overwhelming consequence and will retain a deep fear of disruption and chaos.

It is important to mention that in dealing with catastrophe, the more support one has, and the more informed and empathetic that support is, the easier it will be to manage sudden and precipitously disruptive events. It is not a guarantee against pain and suffering, but the creation of an environment in which one feels understood will lighten their load to a significant degree, albeit never really removing the pain entirely. It can, however, make the painful and cataclysmic moments more tolerable and manageable.

Aging provides opportunities for gaining empathy, wisdom, and knowledge of the world—one would expect those factors to insulate against being overwhelmed and massively traumatized by catastrophe. However, the aging process may include losses of significant others that leave one alone and less supported in crises situations. The older we become, the more likely we are to lose our support systems, unless we have laboriously nurtured a system around us that can serve us well during times of great need. All too often we only realize the need for a significant support system when we are in the midst of crises or catastrophe—by that point it is hard to recruit close others. Thus, it behooves us to nurture a group of others with whom we share our ideas, dreams, knowledge, wisdom, and support, so that in times of need we do not find ourselves alone.

There is also great gratification and enhanced self-esteem that comes from helping others through crises in their lives. Ultimately, the more exposure we have to catastrophe within ourselves, and vicariously through our involvement with others in crises, the more familiar, more prepared, and less apprehensive we will be when it inevitably befalls us.

19

Turning the Corner on Change

I T IS NOT HARD TO see that people make the same mistakes over and over, and it's especially easy to see it in others rather than in yourself. When you do the same thing over and over and expect a different outcome, that is a good way to define insanity. And while that may be true, making changes to basic patterns of behaving and reacting is much easier said than done. We tend to be creatures of habit even though we like to believe we are capable of acting freely, and that our behavior is determined by our conscious mind and choices. But the reality is that most of our behaviors and reactions to recurrent stimuli are essentially predetermined and unconscious. Thus, change is especially difficult because it involves knowing and reexperiencing the unconscious determinants of our behaviors and then making adaptive changes in how we function, through deep and emotional understanding of our motives.

We can understand what motivates us and what seems to determine our behaviors, but just knowing is simply not enough to make specific changes. The critical factor in change is often unknown and non-specific.

For mental health workers at all levels, the most difficult questions are "how will I change" and "what do I have to do to react differently"? The reason for this is that few of us are truly in touch with what motivates our specific reactions to specific stimuli. Shifting long-standing and long-established patterns of behavior is enormously hard to do.

In the field of psychology there is the concept of "repetition compulsion," which usually means that a person will repeat certain patterns of behavior even if, through historical evaluation, those patterns do not work out well and have proven to be ineffective in resolving issues. There appears to be an unconscious wish to master the failed previous attempt, and to have a sense that this time it will work out. And so, we respond as we always do, but this time expect a different outcome. The wish to master a conflict with the same technique is fueled by the narcissistic assault (i.e., pain) of failed previous attempts at solution. And despite our knowing that this manner of attempted resolution did not work, there is a "fatal attraction" to trying it again, in order to prove to ourselves that we can really make this happen. As I stated above, it is one definition of insanity. And, in my opinion, an excellent one!

So, what is it that allows for a change in the stimulus-response pattern? If there is to be adaptive change in long-established patterns of behavior, there must be some key to making that change. We know that a simple understanding of the underlying dynamics of what motivates particular behaviors and response patterns is not enough. Even when there is emotional reexperiencing aspects to our understanding, it does not guarantee change. The missing component required to make that behavioral adaptation is the most difficult question for people in the mental health field to answer honestly and concisely. They are not being evasive; the fact is, they do not really know, and cannot articulate precisely with any sense of assurance, what it is that makes for change. They know they have seen it, and can identify the changes when they do occur, but to pinpoint what it is that makes for the actual change remains largely unknown. What we do know is that change becomes possible when we create a setting for individuals in any therapeutic setting (not only in the therapist's office) and especially if the individual is highly motivated to explore, reflect, and be critical of their past solutions to problems (both successful and unsuccessful). However, we have still not determined what the essential ingredient is in that therapeutic milieu that facilitates change, and what makes the milieu therapeutic at all.

The major characteristic of a therapeutic milieu is that it includes both a person trying to change and another person listening to that person's attempts to change. The person listening and trying to understand will do so without distraction or criticism, with curiosity, and without a need to interrupt or even intervene on the recitation of the person trying to make a change. The listener will not have any investment in any specific change that the person is trying to make, and when the change that needs to occur is obvious, at least to the observer, they will resist making suggestions or giving advice. The listener does not have any deep-seated need for that person to make the change, but he may hope that it can happen—out of empathy and a wish to see another person make adaptive changes in behavior and in self-control.

PART 3
RANDOM PERSPECTIVES

20

Courage and Cowardice

SOMETIMES THE BORDERLINE BETWEEN COURAGE and cowardice is very difficult to distinguish. I think specifically of individuals in relationships when I think of these two seemingly opposite positions. Where relationships work, and the connection between people is harmonious and satisfying, there is very little to decide—we simply want it to continue as is. Why would we want to change something that seems to work and provide gratification on a predictable and consistent basis? It is when relationships, even protracted ones, are not working that the issue of choice arises. Perhaps it is best to ask it this way: what do you do when you realize you find yourself in a situation that simply does not work for you, regardless of whether you've made some serious attempts to change your circumstances for the better? When your conclusion says that this is absolutely not good for you, what do you do then?

We would often say that you must try to work things out, because to do otherwise is to face a judgmental environment that does not approve of a lack of trying. But there are times when you can clearly see that you have come to the end of the road, and it no longer serves your best interests, nor does it satisfy your most basic needs. If you no longer hold out hope for improvement or change, then what?

Is it courageous to opt out of these unsatisfactory connections, even after having made whatever attempts at correction seem appropriate? On the other hand, is it cowardice to stay put, not ever giving yourself the opportunity to find a better solution to your dilemma? My experience has shown me time and time again that many people, if not most, will stay put, and resign themselves to a life of disappointment and disillusionment, rationalizing their lack of courage and mobility by claiming they are "doing the reasonable thing." They desperately try to convince themselves (and perhaps others as well) that they are staying put and doing what is best for others, sacrificing themselves and their futures based on that rationalization. Of serious issue here is that, in order to make a move away from that connection, one is rarely seen as making a powerful, or rational, or meaningful move—instead, it is seen as a decision made without concern or consideration for others involved. The individual who chooses to leave a setting that is frustrating and without meaning or joy, and ultimately self-denying, is far too often seen as negative. Tangential people will all too often see this as a self-centered and egotistical decision, not considering the feelings of others.

Is the person who resigns himself to a life of meaningless activity, all the while servicing the needs of others in his immediate community, not acting out of cowardice? It takes courage to make a move on your own behalf, especially when that move will be judged in a harsh and negative manner by so many others. Do those "others" judge harshly because they themselves may be envious of your decision to move away from frustration and disappointment, and envious in general of the courage you displayed? Those same individuals cannot see themselves ever doing acts of courage and resourcefulness. As a result, they need to forcefully back away from even examining the motives or thought patterns of the person with the courage to stand up for himself and make a move when it suits him.

It not an act of cowardice to stay in a setting that does not provide the pleasure and satisfaction we all seek. And while the rationalization will cover the surface activity (of staying put), that thought pattern, via in-depth perception, will never satisfy, because we know we are sacrificing ourselves for some unclear reason. Even if they cannot articulate that thought, there is an intuitive awareness of selling out. It is much easier to criticize the one who does have the strength of character to make a move when confronted by persistent disappointment and frustration than it is to recognize your own weaknesses and fears. You may have wrapped yourself in the feeling of having acted on a higher plane, but have you really?

My assumption is that, in raising our children, we want to encourage them to be brave, courageous, and have a spirit of adventure. We would be loath to promote cowardness and fearfulness on their part. After all, we believe that an adventuresome spirit will most likely lead a child to more successful heights and enhance their likelihood for happiness and joy in life. And surely, we would feel that being passive or submissive would not be good for the soul and would inhibit success down the road. Yet that kind of courage in adults, as mentioned above, is seen as narcissistic, self-aggrandizing, selfish, and certainly not anything to strive towards. Is there some kind of hypocrisy here? It's acceptable in children, but not in adults? We would never encourage our children to stay with something that was not good for them or required them to be self-sacrificing. In fact we would strongly encourage them to make changes in a more positive direction. We would strongly recommend that they leave negative and disillusioning situations and move towards a more gratifying and pleasurable setting. If that is the case, then why not in adults too?

The issue of sacrifice has been a phenomenon in our history, pretty much from the beginning. God apparently asked Abraham to sacrifice his son Isaac, and Abraham, without much questioning, was quite willing to do that, believing that if he gave up his son, then surely God would reward his people. Today, sacrifice is no longer practiced actively—how much is it endorsed and facilitated passively? We do not look askance at the individual who "sacrifices" for his family; in fact, we look with admiration on that seemingly selfless action, and may even see it as heroic. Certainly, in times of war, the soldier that sacrifices himself to save his fellow soldiers is considered a hero, and perhaps rightly so. In the New Testament of the Bible, John 15:13 tells us, "No greater love has one man than to lay down his life for his fellow man." A beautiful idea and rich in abstract reward, but a very special circumstance where bravery, courage, and selflessness are intimately associated with sacrifice.

Generally speaking, we would not expect or ask for another to lay down his or her life for us. That would seem too entitled, too self-serving, and too narcissistic. And yet we "honor" the person who accepts far less of life and allows himself to be excluded from discovering and enjoying connections that are meaningful and rich—such a difference than what we preach to our children. Instead, we promote in them to not be satisfied with less, and to search out rich and meaningful relationships and opportunities. But we apparently do not promote that in adults. And so, how do we explain this seeming paradox? I fear there is a significant dose of hypocrisy and lack of courage in the answer to that question.

21

The Role of Women

THERE IS A SAYING THAT "behind every great man is a greater woman" that alludes to the influence and power exerted by women. That concept of men needing a powerful, influential, and encouraging woman behind him is not a new one, but the relevance of that role is rarely examined and explained. There are endless examples of how men have been encouraged and propelled to great heights of achievement, and to great discoveries and explorations, based upon being pushed from behind by the women they were involved with.

Every man has been a child at one time and had a mother or at least a "mothering person" in his lifetime. That person may not always have been a woman but was a person that helped him develop and evolve to his adult status. Sometimes, the "mothering person" can be one's father or some other man, but the role is more typical of a maternal influence. That person may not have always been a biological mother but a woman who influenced and encouraged him in his development, such as a grandmother, nanny, or housekeeper. The critical aspect of that role is willingness by the adult to watch over, encourage, and promote good healthy self-esteem in the young child. A child without that influence will more often than not have difficulty in achieving and being a successful and powerful adult.

Sigmund Freud was quoted as saying, "The firstborn son of a young mother carries forever the feeling of a conqueror, and has the greatest likelihood of becoming one." The implication here is that mothering persons who praise and appreciate the talents and abilities of the young child will provide a milieu for that child to grow up in and feel confident. Knowing that his mother feels he is quite special will translate to his feeling quite special himself, particularly where praise and encouragement by that figure has been discriminating and appropriate to his abilities.

Of course, there are exceptions to that "rule," where strength of character and the sense that someone is a special person with special talents is hard to find. What we know for sure is that that self-perception will push that young person to significant levels of achievement, and the source of that push might even remain a mystery.

Even in these times of more female roles in politics, business, medicine, law, and more, women may still be pushed into the background of power positions for a wide variety of reasons. Unfortunately, male dominance in many fields is still very profound, and "pushing through the ceiling" for women is often a complicated, if not impossible, activity. Fortunately, there are many exceptions to that rule, but male dominance in certain areas still persists.

Returning to our original concept of the women behind the men, I do not mean to imply that because women have problems in attaining positions of great power they are then relegated to being the power behind the man as a compensatory move. The ability to sponsor a man is not a role for the weak and fragile, or downtrodden. Quite to the contrary, the "woman behind that man" is often a powerhouse in her own rights, but for whatever reason may not have had the opportunity or option to actively pursue that fame or power on her own accord. One could easily imagine that the woman who pushes her spouse or son or nephew to great achievement might also be able to obtain vicarious pleasure from the success, but it is likely not the motivating reason for her support.

Motherhood, like parenthood in general, involves a wide range of motives. The wish to be influential and encouraging is at the base of being an excellent parent. While there are a significant number of primary functions of parenthood, the role of encouraging one's child to pursue their basic strengths and proclivities is a primary function of parenthood, for both mothers and fathers. To recognize the aspects of your child that you can encourage and facilitate and to know when and how to do that kind of encouragement is a major feat and differentiates good parents from less good parents.

Often, the quality of parenting that parents experience as children will lay down an infrastructure to be followed when they have their own children. This infrastructure and role modeling has been internalized, and will be largely unconscious. The parent who is able to understand the strengths and weaknesses of their parents' parenting styles, and make changes accordingly, is much more likely to be an ideal parent for their own children.

We like to believe that as the generations proceed, quality of parental care will improve. While that may be true, it requires the ability to reflect upon one's own parenting experience as children, and to adapt new and better techniques in those areas where one's parents' parenting may have slipped. Because the style of parenting you experienced is laid down early in one's life, the ability to alter that is a major enterprise.

Altering requires a major upheaval of what you believed was ample and appropriate parenting. It is only later in life that we discover the nature and effectiveness of our personal parenting experience—being honestly critical is not an easy task. It requires you to be able to look at your parents in an objective manner and see what they did that was positive and not so positive. It is only through this kind of examination that changes in your parenting style can be made. The simple recognition of positivity or negativity in your experience with your parents will still necessitate careful examination and insight to make significant change.

In a sense, parents are responsible for establishing a set of realistic goals for their children, based upon careful examination and investigation of their children's interests, talents, and abilities. The degree to which it is actually based upon a child's abilities and not upon the parent's wishes for the child, coming from their own shortcomings in life, the closer to reality and closer to what the child can realistically achieve going forward. A mother, or even a father, who expects too much of a child, for whatever the reasons, will damn that child to a life of disappointment and fear. That child will always be looking over his shoulder wondering what his parent thinks about his performance. He will not be free to utilize his capacities freely. Instead of his experiencing joy in achievement, he will experience only relief, but that relief will not be long-lasting.

There are clear situations where women who do possess great strength of character, intelligence, and fortitude, may consciously choose to abdicate their opportunities in order to serve the role of mother, wife, daughter, or friend. It is not a resignation from success, but because they see that power and success can come through the ability to promote ambition and drive in another. It is not a sign of weakness, and may well be a quality of sacrifice, but for a far higher motive. The ability to help out the person that you "sponsor" in life may bring you tremendous satisfaction—you will know that you have had a major hand in his or her success, and the person you helped will know that without your encouragement and appropriate support, they might not have been able to achieve that level of success.

22

Inner Beauty

THE WORD "BEAUTIFUL" HAS MANY meanings. It can refer to the superficial attributes of a person's persona, and it can relate to the inner beauty found on their less visible aspects. We are inundated with the aspect of beauty in our culture, mainly pertaining to the physical beauty that confronts the eye and seems to separate individuals (probably more often women than men) from one another. It is a well-known axiom "that one man's beauty is another man's poison." In other words, beauty is a matter of high levels of specificity. Each of us defines and recognizes beauty in different ways, depending in large part on our own unique history and past experiences. The appreciation of beauty, especially superficial, is a learned phenomenon. We get our cues for what is beautiful and what is not by a multitude of external hints acquired from watching and dealing with others and their own definitions of "beauty."

But it is the non-physical beauty that is far more interesting and important: the beauty that is within us as individuals, that defines our personalities, interests, and attitudes towards the world and the people in our spheres of influence. Beauty in this aspect is a far more difficult term to define, and like the beauty of the superficial kind, we all have varying attributes which we would define as inner beauty. Our descriptions of inner beauty often relate to the nature of our own personality and our connections and interactions with others. And like the appreciation of skin-deep beauty, the appreciation of inner beauty is a learned phenomenon. If we have not been taught the value and significance of "inner beauty," it would be an irrelevant perception. But once we become aware, and can appreciate the value of an individual with those special qualities, it is hard to steer away from that, and hard to be associated with individuals who lack that quality.

The development of inner beauty is a complicated process. It is not a genetically determined character trait, nor is it hereditary, except that one's heritage and the people who raise you may themselves have aspects of that quality and will surely find some way to communicate it to you. It is certainly not a set of character traits that is easily incorporated or internalized, but instead the development of a sense of empathy, sensitivity to others, generosity of spirit, willingness to give and be available to others in need, and to be a civilized, non-narcissistic individual. It is a slow, step-by-step accretion of a manner and an infrastructure that impacts how we relate to the world around us.

A child growing up in an environment where there are others with that quality of inner beauty and strength will have a far better chance of embracing those same qualities and learning from their role models. Children growing up in an atmosphere of selfishness, greed, lack of empathy, and insensitivity will have a far less likely chance of acquiring those attributes of inner beauty and strength. Often these children (and later as adults) will not recognize their lack of this spirit—they may even categorize individuals with empathic and sensitive skill sets as silly, weak, foolish, lazy, or even stupid. They will be utterly blind to the values of such a personality and character structure. They will not appreciate the joys and rewards of relating to the world around them with civility, empathy, and sensitivity. People who embrace the concepts of "inner beauty" will, in fact, derive significant joy and satisfaction from exercising those attributes and adding to the comfort levels of others around them. They will feel the satisfaction of helping others and doing good work in the world.

"Inner beauty" is clearly a vague concept, yet we all recognize it when it when we see it: assistance and generosity is given without need for repayment or reciprocal care and brings joy to both the giver and the receiver. It may also be the case in certain circumstances that these open-minded and generous people can be taken advantage of, even manipulated, by uncaring and sociopathic types. The person with that "inner beauty" may shrug off the manipulative and selfish acts of their "predators" and not be dissuaded from their original goals with that person. Part of the internal strength of that person is their ability to push on and try to be helpful and generous, even in the face of serious obstacles. It is not that they are foolish, but rather driven to do and be good, and to influence others, even the undeserving, in ways that enhance life for the other individual.

There are exceptions to what I've stated above, namely that children who grow up in an environment with role models that have that inner beauty are more likely to develop similar attributes and attitudes, and those who don't have that modeling will not find a way to develop that inner strength of character. There are instances in which a child may reject what they experience directly and take on attributes in direct opposition to what they have witnessed. For example, the child growing up in a rather negative milieu will sometimes reject what he has seen, and take on more positive attributes and attitudes, figuring it out for himself along the way. These will usually be very interesting and genuine individuals who have worked hard at being different than what they witnessed in others; they find joy and satisfaction in not emulating what they experienced growing up. The opposite can also be found: a child growing up in a very loving and empathic environment may reject that style of interacting and adopt a more aggressive perspective

In these situations, there is usually some deeper explanation as to why the rejection of what they have witnessed drove them in an unusual and unexpected direction. In these cases, there usually has been some trauma and pain suffered that makes an individual veer away from what they know, in either direction.

The nature of the trauma may be totally obscured and hidden, and not even known by the individual himself. But for a child or an adult to take that unexpected direction suggests some disappointing and frightening observations and understandings. Sadly, by the time someone becomes aware of their divergence from their past, it may be too late to change direction. The understanding required to make shifts in basic human attitudes about others is a major task and one that cannot be changed handily or easily.

People are often resistant to exploring and discovering the origins of what caused them to change direction. It requires tremendous strength and serious self-reflection to admit to yourself that you have gone against the grain of your history, even in those instances where the direction has resulted in a more positive outcome. Oppositional positioning usually is accompanied by extreme defensiveness and with a need to rationalize decisions made in opposition.

Those blessed with "inner beauty" will have little need to explore their motives and goals. They will generally be content and happy souls, not needing deep reflection and understanding of their basic nature. Why would one seek hidden answers when their life is being lived in a joyous, satisfying, and happy manner?

23

The Truth About Independence

THE PUSH TOWARDS INDEPENDENCE IS a struggle for all children, and one that can stretch into adulthood, especially where there has been faulty support for the development of independent activity and thought. It is a state we all supposedly strive for, although some of us have massive amounts of ambivalence when it comes to making the move toward independent behaviors.

What is it that we strive to achieve through independent activity and behavior? Healthy adaptive adults seem to make their own decisions and follow their own pathways, less influenced by outsiders. They appear to be happy and content with the decisions they make, and even when they have made errors in judgment. These individuals take great pleasure in following their own leads and inclinations, and do not fear making a mistake. In fact, they learn from them.

This is in sharp contrast with individuals who have aborted independence, or have incomplete and underdeveloped autonomous decision-making capacities. These individuals will be hesitant to make their own decisions and will often require the advice or counsel of others before they proceed. Even when they have chosen a direction for themselves, they will do so with caution and apprehension, and without a feeling of confidence. They will be easily wounded and intensely self-castigating if they make an even inconsequential mistake.

Perhaps the essence of independent activity is the ability to be confident in one's decisions, and to not have the totality of one's self-esteem hinged to any particular decision or activity. Independent thinking assumes resilience and flexibility—and the ability to change direction if necessary—without self-criticism or self-punishment. The lack of an independent identity is characterized by uneasiness, unsureness, ambivalence, and an inability to shift and change based upon self-reflection and self-recognition.

Adolescence is the primary period of time when the drive for independence exhibits itself most dramatically—but it is not limited to that period of life. Independence of thought and activity is a set of feelings and actions that begin much earlier, occurring even before being able to verbally communicate. The ability of a child to make certain decisions for himself, even if the decisions are simple in nature, are intimately connected to the willingness and ability of his parents to allow for that. Parents who control their child more than what would be considered the norm will interfere with their child's development regarding independent thoughts and action. The willingness of parents to allow for that phase to occur is absolutely critical in their child's ability to achieve that state of mind and feeling on their own. A child who has suffered too much at the hands of one or more "helicopter" parents will clearly have difficulty in the achieving and accepting of independence. He will not be able to make independent decisions or take autonomous direction. The feeling and difficulty will persist long after that child's parents are directly involved in his day-to-day life. And sadly, that same child will always look for direction, and feel uneasy when left to his own devices. Additionally, he will tend to connect with others who are only willing to direct, counsel, and force him in one way or another, according to their wishes, even if it is to his detriment. He will never feel that sense of freedom and self-esteem that comes from being one's own person, making certain decisions for oneself, regardless of outcome.

Additionally, the child who has received too much direction from others will feel a sense of deprivation, but may never really know why. He will feel the uneasiness of being left to his own decision-making, but will not process it in such a way as to strike out on his own, daring to take the chance of making a mistake or taking a wrong turn. He will not be resilient when left to himself to direct and make his way, especially if he sees that he has made an error or exercised faulty judgment. He may even be wracked with serious indecision when on his own, choosing to do nothing instead of taking a chance on being wrong. Parents who tend to hover will also be critical of mistakes their child has made when they were not involved in that child's decision. Thus, that child will often find himself frozen and unable to move forward because he does not feel comfortable making his own decisions and becomes immobilized, fearful of making a mistake and being criticized for it, even when the criticism comes from within.

Then there is the child who has been given the appropriate license to make his own decisions and grows up feeling more and more confident about his ability to decide for himself. If his parents or other authorities have not hovered, nor been critical of his past decisions, he will then feel resilient, even when things do not work out perfectly for him. His parents will have made allowances for mistakes and will have praised his efforts in trying things, rather than judging the outcome of his attempts at independence. He will have been optimally frustrated over time and had the opportunity to learn that things do not always turn out as he hoped they would, but he will know that experience does not dictate his entire self-worth. Great value will have been given to his efforts and attempts at success—his failure was not because he did not listen to his parents, but because "sometimes it just works out that way." When something doesn't work out, he will be encouraged to explore why, and to correct it, but will not be made to feel that he is an utter failure because this one endeavor did not work out.

We can easily see why, in this case, the child who has had some free rein to explore, make decisions as well as mistakes, and feel good about his efforts, will eventually feel good about himself. He will develop confidence in his ability to make things happen for himself, and not be distracted from his goals and ideals should something not work out as planned.

Then there is the other child who has been left alone too much and expected to decide everything for himself. From early on, he learned there was no one to turn to for help and advice, and that no one appears to care about his outcome and feelings of self-worth. This child will often develop a sense of what I describe as "pseudo-independence." The term implies that while an individual may appear to act on an independent basis, in truth he is only pretending. Because he has been left on his own, he must develop and nurture concepts on his own, without any guidance. In some areas he will overshoot autonomy; in others he may wildly undershoot independent action. He will struggle with being confident about his decision-making, but will never let on that he is unsure—he suffers with a fragile ego, one that is easily bruised.

This individual may appear oppositional in nature: if told to go right, he goes left. If told to jump up, he jumps down. While this may appear to be self-directed behavior, in fact, he is being directed by others. If we tell him to go right and he goes to the left (in order to be in opposition) then he is still being directed by our instruction. His turning left is not autonomous, but rather a dependent action (i.e., dependent upon what he is told from without). This person will have serious self-doubts, and even if he looks like he is making his own decisions, he is often directed from the outside, as in the examples above. The absence of optimal frustration, as in the second individual we discussed, will lead him to be a bit helter-skelter when it comes to goals, motivations, and actions. He may behave erratically and impulsively, and his self-esteem and self-confidence may be volatile and unpredictable. He will no doubt be attracted to other individuals of the same ilk, because in their similar actions and motivations, they will not question one another, and instead will defend one another's activities.

The issue of optimal frustration is central to the whole concept of the development of truly independent action. The timely acceptance of responsibility for one's decisions, without criticism for errors and a feeling of support for trying to make things happen for oneself, will ultimately yield a much more autonomous individual. However, it takes parents or other authorities with empathy and understanding to know when to back off and when to intervene to avoid catastrophe. The idea that we learn from our mistakes is a powerful truism, but only when there is an atmosphere of support and encouragement. Persons with fragile egos or volatile self-esteem will not be resilient in this arena. Their egos will react strongly to making errors, and they will become even more reluctant to act or try new ventures or endeavors, thus increasingly avoiding independent thinking and actions.

The person with fragile self-esteem cannot be wrong: he cannot learn new things, or make adjustments in his thinking, because to do so is to admit and acknowledge weakness or lack of knowledge or understanding, something to be avoided at all costs. To learn and to change, even in a positive direction, takes humility and the willingness to "not know." Without the comfort and acceptance of not knowing, change becomes impossible, and therefore so does further accretion of independent activity and thought.

This latter individual will make a difficult friend or colleague, because his need to be right and to defend his position even in the face of contrary evidence makes cooperation and team play impossible. It will be impossible for him to adjust his thinking, and exhausting for those trying to work with him. He is best avoided, because his presence will make progress, change, and greater understanding excessively difficult and frustrating for everyone else.

24

Making Choices:
How Do You Know When It's Right?

PROBABLY THE MOST COMPLICATED AND impactful choices we ever make in our lives have to do with choosing relationships with lovers, friends, colleagues, and associates of any kind. How do we know when it is right? Can you even know at the onset when it is right? What we clearly know is that you can surely figure out when it is wrong, right from the get-go. The signs that lead one to know that a relationship is not a fit are often much more obvious than those that determine a relationship that is right. And what is right can change over time and based on experience, making it that much harder to make effective, long-lasting choices.

The critical factor in making correct choices, especially when it comes to choosing people that we allow to get close to us, has to do with how well we know ourselves, how familiar we are with what we are looking for, and our awareness of the traps we might fall into. We know these traps (or should) from our experiences in the past. Theoretically, we all have certain features we share with others that will attract us, as well as certain features which will repel us. The extent to which we are familiar and at ease with our own self-knowledge, and the criteria that make us attracted to—or rejecting of—others, will ultimately determine the nature and effectiveness of our choices.

The problem arises when we do not recognize recurrent patterns within our own behavior. We do not question repeated failures and faulty choices we make in establishing relationships. Instead, we are blindly attracted by the same attributes over and over again, not recognizing that there is more to the person than the initial presentation, and that their choices are too often made upon superficial and fleeting aspects of the personality of the other person. The blindness is in not seeing that there is a repeating, eventually self-punitive effect that arises from the choices we make. And so there is never the motivation to question or be curious about why this has not worked out...again. In this scenario, we are doomed to repeat our errors in judgment and will continue to make faulty choices, hoping (against hope) that this time it will turn out differently.

We say that to know oneself and to know what it is that we are looking for is the key to making better choices—this pertains to all areas of life, not just relationships. The only way to know what we look for and what attracts us, and what turns us off, is to be curious as to why someone interests us while someone else does not. To be instantly interested in another, without time to explore, understand, or get to know that person and their particular attributes and attitudes, is a formula for disaster. So many relationships and associations amongst people begin with the thinnest of investigation and curiosity, and are initiated by superficial and perhaps even meaningless attributes of each other. The key is the presence of patience, discrimination, and the ability to delay jumping into something new without evaluation—often motivated by the presence of a deep need that needs to be superficially met in short order. This is a formula for future disaster. The less discriminating the choice, the less likely there is to be success in the relationship, no matter the nature of the connection.

So, knowing yourself and your interests is absolutely critical, as is also being intimately aware of your weaknesses and your tendencies to choose poorly in certain instances. Without that type of intimate self-knowledge, how does one become aware of these aspects of one's proclivities, in order to avoid the mistakes that are possible? It is solely established through the repeated evaluation and curiosity, and self-observation, of oneself in action, particularly in respect to dealing with others. When this kind of careful self-examination occurs on a repeated basis, and in a variety of circumstances (both positive and negative), a slow accretion of self-understanding and self-awareness will become available for measuring and determining the rightness or wrongness of a particular connection with somebody new. It is a serious need to rely upon the inner voice we all have; a voice that many of us are not trained or inclined to rely upon.

The tendency to repeat foolish choices, particularly when it comes to choosing love relationships, is a frequent phenomenon. If the criteria for making specific choices are more superficial and less examined, the likelihood of faulty choices dramatically increases. And where there is less self-examination and less self-awareness, and where the criteria for choices are flimsy and superficial, how likely is it to make a choice that will work out?

One would think that people would adjust their choice making based upon the outcome of former choices, especially where the choices were not so effective and gratifying. But in these circumstances, self-esteem creeps in and rather than being able to see the folly of ones' former choices, there will often be a tendency to rationalize and justify them instead. In this case, we make choices in order to save face and preserve a feeling of self-esteem and confidence. To be able to accept your mistakes, and do it without self-castigation, allows for the possibility of change and the opportunity to move forward. And while this is especially in this arena of love relationships, it is true in relationships of all types: the ability to accept one's faulty logic and examine the motivations and determinants for making that choice is a step in the direction of correction and making better choices for oneself in the future.

At times, it is astonishing to chart the choices that people make over time. It often appears that there is little or no self-observation, and little or no curiosity about what motivates or determines certain behaviors and choices. While the determinants to behavior of all kinds are based upon unconscious factors and are outside the conscious awareness of the individual, by repeated self-observation and questioning of the motives of certain behaviors one can infer the unconscious determinants of one's actions. The conscious awareness of what determines your behaviors, even if they are not immediately palpable or visible, can facilitate the beginning of change in a more healthful and helpful direction.

People who believe that their activities and behaviors are determined by conscious will, and by their conscious direction, will not be amenable to this kind of change. In fact, the concept of unconscious determination feels like an insult to them, as if they are not under control, which of course they are not. It is narcissistically assaultive to them to admit that reality to themselves.

Is there anything that can be done to alter or correct the blindness that overtakes someone who fails to have curiosity about their poor choices? In the field of psychology, we often say that a person has to "want to make change" before it can happen, and even then it is a difficult task. Thus, unless these "blind" individuals find themselves in an environment with a trusted other—a parent, friend, close colleague, or even a partner—they will be reluctant to face the "poor and faulty choices" they have made. But if they can be encouraged to explore and examine the motives and directives they have (unconsciously) followed in an atmosphere of non-judgment and non-criticism, and in a supportive way, they just might take a serious look at their inner workings. In doing so, and in discovering the faulty logic they have used in the past to choose their connections with others, they open the possibility for a dramatic change in decision- and choice making. But the atmosphere and trusting environment must be consistent, predictable, and infinitely available for this to be effective. And even when these criteria are met, there is no absolute guarantee that change will occur.

Ultimately it is the sensitivity and vulnerability of their self-esteem that determines their willingness to explore these issues in depth and without self-denigration. It is never easy for us to openly examine our own faults and foolish choices, but it is absolutely necessary if we want productive change. Otherwise, without the courage and persistence to self-evaluate, we are doomed to repeat the same ridiculous choices, with the same negative outcome.

25

To Choose or not to Choose

MAKING A CHOICE IS A CRITICAL decision. The ability to choose and know what's best is not always an easy task, and choosing involves consequences. Some of our choices have an enormous impact on the rest of our lives. For example, choosing a career, spouse, business partner, or close friend can have a significant bearing on us now and in the future. To choose poorly, and without discrimination, opens us to problems down the road, even if they are not evident when we initially make them. How many times have we all heard and even thought to ourselves, "What was I thinking?"

Of course, we are all smart and clever when we look back with the retro-spectroscope. Of course, we have all made choices and decisions that come back to haunt us and clearly were not what we were expecting. It is also true that certain choices have to be made at times when we are less informed, and less able to realistically understand and examine all the vicissitudes and variables of a certain choice. The best example is when we have to decide about a life direction—we're often very young when we're asked to decide what we are going to be and do with our lives. The decision to be a doctor, lawyer, businessperson, or teacher are all choices we are expected to make before we really know the world around us, or where we truly fit into it. Unfortunately, our choices often end up in disappointment or frustration because we did not really know what that choice entailed or would mean for us. And that same concept (of choosing before we are well-informed) pertains to other choices we make early in life, ones that can dramatically affect our lives. Our choice of a spouse, business partner, or close friend may backfire over time because the criteria we used to make that choice was naïve, foolish, or impulsive.

The ability to make reasoned choices is obviously impacted by both time and experience. But it is also a matter of self-assurance and self-confidence. Experience is vitally necessary in making choices both early on and later as we develop and as we mature and are able to make increasingly complex choices for ourselves. Even very young children will have the opportunity to make choices, if given the license to do so. The child who is not given the license early on, and especially later on when decisions and choices become more critical and important, will struggle making those choices. The parent or authority who needs to be in control of the child beyond what is reasonable and expected will stunt and disturb that child's ability to make his own choices with confidence and assurance. From an early age, he will be uneasy with the choices he makes, and will need to "check things out first" with the controlling parent. He will either not make choices or freeze when asked to make a decision. He might be prone to making impulsive choices to rid himself of the anxiety of choosing. He will worry constantly that his choices are foolish or wrong and will be increasingly hesitant to choose when the opportunity arises.

The parent or authority who allows the child to make easy decisions for himself (without being critical of that child's choices) and supportive of choices made that don't work out so well will create a milieu in which that child will be able to explore, evaluate, and carefully consider what he wants the outcome to be, and how best to achieve that outcome. He will not be frozen and fearful of being wrong but will understand that mistakes happen, and that those mistakes do not define who he is or the value and worth he contributes.

26

Prognosticating the Future

DOES IT REALLY HAPPEN THAT some of us are gifted in certain ways, such that we can accurately and predictably forecast the future and what will eventually happen? We all know individuals like that—people who swear they have this rare ability to know what will happen before it actually does. It is easy to scoff at the idea because it seems irrational: how could one realistically know what is about to occur? And yet there are people who truly believe they can tell the future with reasonable accuracy. Is there some magic they possess? Do they possess some ability to look into a crystal ball and forecast future events, whether that prediction is of an individual or the world in general? Or is it that they have a way of weaving what actually does happen into something that already took place? Clearly, it is a powerful and narcissistically-gratifying attribute, one that will garner all kinds of accolades and praise from others.

While it is true that we all have certain kind of premonitions, these premonitions are based upon a percentage likelihood of certain events occurring. For example, if we go to a baseball game, and the league-leading team is playing against the league cellar-dwelling team, it may not be such an unreasonable premonition to predict that the cellar-dweller will lose that game. In instances like this, you will be right much of the time. But was that really foreseeing the future? Or was it a premonition based upon studying the facts of the situation?

Similarly, if a person is diagnosed with a critical (perhaps even terminal) disease, how much of a premonition is it to feel that that person will soon die? And when they do die at some point, is it really an ability to foretell the future to have made that prediction?

There are other scenarios where a person may have a certain foreboding sense that something negative or positive is about to happen. How do we explain that experience when the thing that is being anticipated actually occurs? Is it really prognosticating the future, or is it a common understanding that underlies our ability to make general statements that appear to predict the future? It is a mystery to many of us how traditional fortune-tellers are able to make predictions—about people they have never seen or talked to—that seem to eventually come true by just asking some basic information, such as a birthdate or age. For the person for whom the prediction has been made, it may be that the truth is based upon their own perceptions. But is this really foretelling the future, and is this teller of fortunes really accurately and reliably seeing the future?

One would have to admit that there must be some trick to this, since we do not reasonably accept that this fortune-teller can predict outcomes for a person they do not know in any in-depth manner. But what is this trick? And is this trick the same for the person who seems to believe that they can sense a future outcome of some event or personal crisis?

Perhaps the real trick lies in the willingness and eagerness of individuals involved. The teller of fortunes understands and knows this. Thus, in making predictions, and couching them as premonitions, fortune-tellers make generalizations that could apply to a wide range of people in a wide range of experiences—and because individuals want to believe, they do. Because the wish to want to believe the fortune-teller is so powerful, we rationalize the events that do happen (whether negative or positive), so they coincide with the predictions of the soothsayer. And when the events that eventuate are different than what was predicted, we easily forgive the fortune-teller for not being 100 percent correct— how could they have really known?

The wish to be known and understood lies at the base of future prognostications. To clearly acknowledge a difference in what actually happened from what was predicted is a painful and dystonic feeling of isolation and loneliness—every effort is made to make the possible connection between outcome and prediction, in order to protect self-esteem and to avoid the feeling of being unknown.

Why do we feel so skeptical about individuals who claim to be able to predict future events? We quickly want to state that there is no way a person can realistically foretell the future. The concept goes against the grain of our sense of reality, and may even rub us the wrong way. The idea of people having some supernatural abilities that we ourselves may not possess is a bit of a narcissistic blow to our self-esteem. It perhaps stirs some sense of envy—why them and not me? This is a perfectly understandable reaction to witnessing something positive in another that we are not capable of. The instinctive urge is to question or doubt their ability.

It may even explain the easy and quick rejection of the whole concept of foretelling the future. We can easily rationalize our position of doubt by claiming it is an irrational idea, but perhaps the real issue is that we are angry that the other person possesses something we don't have. Or at least he appears to have it and we don't. The fact that other individuals may believe and even admire the teller of fortunes, by whatever means used, stirs envy that the teller receives admiration and applause, while we do not. It's so much easier to rely on logic and reality testing than to acknowledge our own vulnerability given that particular "skill" or any other skill set for that matter.

It is possible that this issue of fortune-telling and the skepticism it draws from most of us is that it relies on being able to react positively to the positive attributes of others, which can be a particularly difficult thing for many people. It is a mark of narcissistic vulnerability to have trouble praising or admiring, or even acknowledging the obvious strengths of another person. To recognize and admire another requires a sense of emotional and psychological balance in the individual doing the admiring. A vulnerable and fragile personality will be totally unable to provide that kind of reaction to the positive strengths of others. Thus, the skepticism about "soothsayers" may evidence a much deeper sense of vulnerability, beyond just questioning the absolute truth and reality of the activity.

27

Never Again

IN FEBRUARY OF 2020, I read an article entitled "Auschwitz 75" on the CBS News site that talked about the experiences of several remaining concentration camp survivors returning to the camp grounds of their childhoods, including interviews with them and their reactions to being back there after so many years. Auschwitz was liberated by the Russians in 1945—after the Germans ran for their lives in hopes of escaping being slaughtered by the angry Russian soldiers. What the Russians found there is by now well established history.

Growing up in Canada (I was born in 1940), I was nine or ten before news began to emerge about what had really transpired in the concentration camps of Europe between 1939 and 1945. The entire Jewish community was exposed to what had transpired, and my parents were aghast and sickened at the news. We heard what seemed like absolutely unbelievable and horrifying stories recounting torture, starvation, illness, and brutality unlike any other, such as Dr. Mengele's medical experiments.

There was so much death, endless suicides, self-destruction, insanity, and human misery. How did this happen in what had seemed like a civilized world? At a certain level, one can understand war—people shooting at each other from trenches during World War I—but this kind of insane and beyond-brutal death-dealing seemed utterly unheard of before. Genocide was certainly not a new phenomenon, but of this magnitude? How could you explain it and how could a nation populated by celebrated musicians, poets, writers of all kinds, artists, scientists, and more come to this?

Despite a plethora of seemingly cogent explanations of how this could happen to a nation of cultured, intelligent, and creative people, I do not believe that any satisfying explanation exists, even today. Thus, does the possibility of this happening again persist? Absolutely, though perhaps not in Germany (despite its seemingly aggressive nature with two World Wars to its credit, so far). Since the Holocaust of WWII, we have seen genocide in Rwanda, Vietnam, a wide range of African nations, including Darfur, and more. The rise of another megalomaniac with some messianic and charismatic attributes could perhaps turn a nation to that kind of behavior. In Europe and to a certain extent in North America, we have seen increasing hate crimes against African Americans, Jews, Hispanics, and Asians—many apparently accepted and even ignored.

Teaching about the Holocaust is outlawed in a number of European countries because of the increasing number of Muslims that suggest the nonexistence of this event. In a recent and somewhat stunning poll in the U.S., less than 50 percent of the population knew about the Holocaust and 20 percent had never heard of Auschwitz. We are instructed to remember what happened so that "never again" is firmly established in our minds. Maybe that is true for the descendants of those Jews, Poles, Serbs, Gypsies, and homosexuals that were needlessly slaughtered in the Holocaust, but what of the rest of the world?

My wish here is to examine, if that is even possible, and present some acceptable idea of what it might have felt like as a concentration camp victim or survivor. To simplify that idea in any manner would be an absolute travesty.

One of the survivors interviewed for the article mentioned above talked of constant fear and panic; the ever present feeling that life could end at any moment for you, your parent, your bedmate, your friend. It is close to impossible for most of us to relate or empathize with that feeling. We have all known anxieties, but very few of us have known catastrophic tension and fear to the extent, and with that chronicity, that these concentration camp survivors have. The ever present dangers of death, torture, starvation, and loss are more than most of us can truly understand. The interviewee also mentioned that even some seventy-five years later she still has flashbacks and replays scenarios from within her experiences at Auschwitz. These memories and flashbacks are always associated with sadness, fear, and tension.

In a conversation with world-renowned psychologist Bruno Bettelheim many years ago (while I was a student at the University of Chicago) he noted that the only way to have emotionally and psychologically survived the concentration camp experience was to have become psychotic by completely removing oneself from the reality of the moment and the situation, because to have done otherwise was to have to deal with the magnitude of the horror. He reported that the suicide rate amongst the inmates was enormous. To focus on the reality of their situation, and to be aware of ever present overwhelming danger, was too much for the average psyche to tolerate, such that suicide was a far better solution.

The development of a unique type of PTSD is found in close to 100 percent of survivors, including those in concentration camps such as Auschwitz. It is a type of PTSD found in situations where individuals suffer with chronic, repetitive, overwhelming, and catastrophic feelings, against which they feel utterly and totally impotent and defenseless. These cases of long-standing and persistent PTSD (sometimes over many decades, as in the Holocaust survivors) prove to be extraordinarily resistant to usual psychotherapy and therapeutic techniques. It is also an established fact that these survivors generally do not come to treatment. For those who do, it is usually not for treatment of their long-standing past PTSD, but rather for the emotional and psychological stresses that ordinary non-survivors suffer, such as anxiety, depression, and phobias.

To empathize with the overwhelming fear that we can only imagine these individuals had to endure on a minute-by-minute basis—all the while struggling with the loss of loved ones, any potential "future," as well as productive and satisfying lives—is nearly impossible. Perhaps that fact contributes to the difficulty of therapy, in that the treater cannot truly know and empathize with the pain, fear, loss, and infinite suffering of these individuals.

While it may be hard or impossible to make lives better for these victims, they have found ways to feel better. By simply surviving, and by having children and grandchildren, they symbolically fight back against the vicious and maniacal wish of their captors to exterminate them and remove any trace of "their kind" from the world. Survival and the continuation of their history and memories is victory of the highest order. To be sure, in most cases, while the progeny of the perpetrators may feel guilt or shame over the behavior of their fathers and grandfathers, and retain a wish to make amends, there may still be those with remaining animosity who rationalize the unheard of cruelty and barbarism of their forbearers.

It is therefore necessary to keep the stories fresh in the minds of those who will listen, even if there exists a world that would deny the Holocaust for their own narcissistic and hostile reasons. My hope is that an informed world will be capable of hearing the truth and being appalled by the deniers, liars, and nonbelievers, and feel honestly and deeply, "never again."

ABOUT THE AUTHOR

Leonard D. Elkun, MD, is a psychoanalyst and psychiatrist who has been in private practice since 1972. He has treated many individuals of all ages, and has addressed a variety of different areas of focus within the field of psychiatry.

After finishing a residency in psychiatry at the University of Chicago in 1970, and spending two years on staff in the Department of Psychiatry at the University, he began his private practice and has been active in that endeavor since then. In 1970 he began psychoanalytic training at the Chicago Institute of Psychoanalysis, completing that in 1976.

Dr. Elkun has worked in drug addiction facilities in the Chicago area for many years and has also spent time treating eating disorders in a wide range of ages. Since 1993, he has worked with the geriatric population in assisted living facilities in Illinois, primarily in the treatment of dementia. He remains very active in dealing with medical-legal cases, having made the diagnosis and treatment of individuals suffering with Post-Traumatic Stress Disorder (PTSD), a major focus of his forensic work.

Throughout these different areas of focus, his main interest has always been in adult psychotherapy and psychoanalysis. He has brought the theories and strategies of those modes of treatment to his day-to-day work in each sphere of interest. Both psychiatric training and psychoanalytic thoughts have shaped his attitudes and understanding of the world.

Dr. Elkun's first book, *The Hidden Treasures Within: On Wisdom and Other Essays,* was published in 2019.

www.ingramcontent.com/pod-product-compliance
Lightning Source LLC
LaVergne TN
LVHW021342080426
835508LV00020B/2073